Sing to the LORD with thanksgiving;
   make melody to our God on the lyre!
He covers the heavens with clouds;
   he prepares rain for the earth;
   he makes grass grow on the hills.
He gives to the beasts their food,
   and to the young ravens that cry.
His delight is not in the strength of the horse,
   nor his pleasure in the legs of a man,
but the LORD takes pleasure in those who fear him,
   in those who hope in his steadfast love.

Psalm 147

ELEVATING
GOD

Rick Furmanek

Light Chaser Press
www.lightchaserpress.com

Elevating God

Published by Light Chaser Press

PO Box 2194

Gilbert, Arizona 85299

www.lightchaserpress.com

Copyright © 2012 by Rick Furmanek

All rights reserved

Cover design: by Rick Furmanek

Cover and content photography: © by Rick Furmanek

All rights reserved.

Scripture quotations are from The ESV® Bible (The Holy Bible, English Standard Version®), copyright ©2001 by Crossway. Used by permission. All rights reserved.

Italics indicate emphasis added.

ISBN 978-0-9883499-0-2

First printing, 2012

Also available in eBook and audio

Printed in the United States of America

A special thanks to four women whose godly examples continue to impact my life in so many amazing ways:

Robin, Midge, Judy & Teresa

"And in the last days it shall be," God declares,
"that I will pour out my Spirit on all flesh,
and your sons and your daughters shall prophesy,
    and your young men shall see visions,
    and your old men shall dream dreams;
even on my male servants and female servants
    in those days I will pour out my Spirit, and they shall
prophesy."

Acts 2

For "Bopper"
June 19, 1957 - August 15, 2011

I lift up my eyes to the hills.
　　From where does my help come?
My help comes from the LORD,
　　who made heaven and earth.

He will not let your foot be moved;
　　he who keeps you will not slumber.
Behold, he who keeps Israel
　　will neither slumber nor sleep.

The LORD is your keeper;
　　the LORD is your shade on your right hand.
The sun shall not strike you by day,
　　nor the moon by night.

The LORD will keep you from all evil;
　　he will keep your life.
The LORD will keep
　　your going out and your coming in
　　from this time forth and forevermore.

Psalm 121

Table of Contents

Thus says the LORD: "Let not the wise man boast in his wisdom, let not the mighty man boast in his might, let not the rich man boast in his riches, but let him who boasts boast in this, that he understands and knows me, that I am the LORD who practices steadfast love, justice, and righteousness in the earth. For in these things I delight, declares the LORD."

Jeremiah 9

PREFACE . . .

why I write

It is of no small coincidence that for the last two decades I have found myself on a life-trek through the desert Southwest. My decision to move to Arizona in the late '80's ended up coinciding with a spiritual journey that actually began in early 1990, where I was cast out onto my own personal desert of sorts, thus launching a wilderness expedition that would last some fifteen years.

It was during this period of personal seclusion and acute spiritual restlessness that God first began to gently expose erroneous notions I had come to believe about myself. Because he loved me so, God could no longer permit me to recklessly embrace these deceptive self-perceptions. What I thought about me had to be confronted, seen for what it was, dealt with, and eventually healed. Praise his name; the healing has come.

It was also in my desert experience where I encountered God in a way that I had not previously known him. As the months of inner solitude and reflection turned into years, I gradually began to see that my so-called spiritual life was really made up of nothing more than thinking accurately, speaking correctly, and doing properly. Looking back, this approach had only resulted in a sterile and listless association with God. The condition of my faith was at best, spiritually antiseptic, and at worst, sufficient grounds for disqualification.

The reality of my rather bland and tame view of God hit me quite hard. Having been previously trained in one of the finest seminaries in the Country, and having preached and taught the Bible countless times over the years, I found the gravity of my own spiritual condition utterly embarrassing. But thanks be to such a kind and gracious God; in due time, that embarrassment was transformed into personal conviction . . . a 'godly sorrow' so to speak. It was under God's firm and loving hand that I began to recognize how he had supernaturally orchestrated every single step of my desert journey. God finally had me exactly where he wanted me . . . desperate for him; thus, I write.

October, 2012
Rick Furmanek

xiii

ACKNOWLEDGMENTS . . .

thank you!

The formation of this book could not have come about without the support and insight of key people God strategically placed into my life.

To my readers—Wink, Larry, Midge, Kike, Bob, Mary, Duane, and Sylvia—I cannot begin to express my depth of gratitude for your commitment to the very end. Thank you for your sacrifice of time and effort. Your labors have not been in vain.

To my editors—Judy, Robin, Darryl, Brian, Jennifer, and Lisa—I am deeply indebted to you for your willingness to share, not only your expertise, but also your candid feedback with such a tender spirit, desiring that I only do my very best. You have been an invaluable source of inspiration for me to continue pressing forward.

To the others who have encouraged me, I want to thank you publically for your endearing words of affirmation as I labored to birth this work. May our great God be glorified through every page.

Thus says the LORD:
"Stand by the roads, and look,
  and ask for the ancient paths,
where the good way is; and walk in it,
  and find rest for your souls."
Jeremiah 6

XV

INTRODUCTION . . .

the premise

This book is intended to assist anyone who finds himself or herself in a pursuit for what truly matters in life. It is not a lofty theological work, but it does possess theology—theology being defined as the 'study of God.' It is not intended to convince skeptics, but it will challenge a person's estimation of God. It is not a philosophical work, but it tackles a bit of modern thought. It is not a scientific book, but it does query some science. It is not an apologetic, but it does offer valid reasons to believe. It is not a course on Christianity 101, but it does discuss points that are central to the Christian faith.

With that said, *Elevating God* is an endeavor to spotlight key truths found in the Bible that can help establish a clearer understanding of why God must be preeminent in one's life in order for his or her existence to have true significance.

For some, this may be a new way of looking at God. In present-day Christian klatsches we are often encouraged to direct our focus primarily onto what God can do for us. While receiving from God what is good and necessary for life has great value, I would advocate that the key to experiencing one's true purpose must first begin with a single-minded quest to learn what matters to God. That is the mission of this book, to make God known.

The blueprint of *Elevating God* is rather straightforward. It begins with a basic introduction to God. By exploring what he says of himself we gain a better understanding of how God wants to be seen and known. Then for the next eight chapters we examine what God has done, what God is like, and how God works. The final chapter unfolds the challenge set before us: to speak clearly, to represent truthfully, and to live authentically for God.

At the end of each chapter there is a brief Recalibration section, summing up what has been addressed by way of a challenge to put into operation what you have read. Discussion Questions are also provided for facilitating further personal and/or group study.

This foundational approach is the premise of *Elevating God*. I believe that it is only by a vigilant undertaking to learn what God has told us about himself that we can begin to know what is truly important to him. May this book serve as a catalyst for your own personal recalibration, a spiritual retuning of your life as it were, by challenging you to become first and foremost enraptured with God, the source of all grace and truth.

The sum of your word is truth
Psalm 119

Ah, Lord GOD! It is you who have made the heavens and the earth by your great power and by your outstretched arm! Nothing is too hard for you.

Jeremiah 32

The Perfect Storm - Roswell, New Mexico

Behold, to the LORD your God belong heaven and the heaven of heavens, the earth with all that is in it.

Deuteronomy 10

1

THERE IS NO OTHER . . .

the one true God

For any person who would have a proclivity to search for God, a willingness to believe is integral. In order to encounter him, the Bible asserts that a person's state of unbelief must be first transformed into a life of expectant faith. Remarkably, for the one who chooses to believe, he or she will also discover the marvelous truth that wonderful things are in store for anyone who would pursue him. Hebrews 11:6 says: "And without *faith* it is impossible to please him, for whoever would draw near to God *must believe that he exists* and that he rewards those who seek him."

Attempts to discover God in the laboratory, in academic think tanks, or in an archaeological dig site might yield interesting facts, but without the element of personal faith involved, the quest for God will never reach a satisfying destination. The pursuit of answers regarding the origin and the sustaining of life will continually elude a person. In fact, a life without faith actually suppresses the ability to know the reality of God.

The necessity of faith, as prescribed by the writer of Hebrews, is not a blind faith where one must leap into an idea, ascend an ethereal plane, or enter into a state of spiritual self-awareness in order to locate God. No, the faith spoken of here is built upon the historical evidence of the one true God who is sovereignly in control over all things, and the conviction that he is actively at work both in the seen and unseen world. We are instructed to place our confidence in this God who is unlimited, and works all things according to his plan. This type of faith is authentic, evidential, and operational.

Everything we know about God has come by way of what he himself has chosen to reveal to us. Fortunately, God has told us quite a bit. From just a cursory glance at what goes on in and around us, it is quite clear that he is not hiding from his creation, nor is he playing games with people. God wants us to know him, but how we arrive at that knowledge must be on his terms and not on ours.

So where do we start in our discovery of what God is like? In this culture of chaos, relativism, neo-atheism, hedonism, and narcissism, any personal idea of what God might be like, what God may look like, or what God will do, must always defer to God's own definition of himself.

The Declarative Aspect of God

What has God declared of himself? It is clear from Scripture that God intends to remove all doubt regarding exactly who he is. Here are a few passages that depict him speaking directly to his people regarding his own identity:

> "You are my witnesses," declares the LORD, "and my servant whom I have chosen, that you may know and

believe me and understand that I am he. *Before me no god was formed, nor shall there be any after me. I, I am the LORD, and besides me there is no savior.* I declared and saved and proclaimed, when there was no strange god among you; and you are my witnesses," declares the LORD, "and *I am God.*" (Isaiah 43:10-12)

For thus says the LORD, who created the heavens (he is God!), who formed the earth and made it (he established it; he did not create it empty, he formed it to be inhabited!): "*I am the LORD, and there is no other.*" (Isaiah 45:18)

"Turn to me and be saved, all the ends of the earth! *For I am God, and there is no other.*" (Isaiah 45:22)

"Remember this and stand firm, recall it to mind, you transgressors, remember the former things of old; for *I am God, and there is no other; I am God, and there is none like me,*" (Isaiah 46:8-9)

"You shall eat in plenty and be satisfied, and praise the name of the LORD your God, who has dealt wondrously with you. And my people shall never again be put to shame. You shall know that I am in the midst of Israel, and that *I am the LORD your God and there is none else.* And my people shall never again be put to shame." (Joel 2:26-27)

God has unapologetically declared that he is, not only the one true God, but also the God who can be found by his creation. He assures us that all these other so-called gods are mere 'impotent imitations.' One could say in this particular case, 'imitation is *not* the sincerest form of flattery.' God alone owns the right to be God. This truth is also affirmed by

God's self-disclosure of key traits that reside solely in him. We will examine three of those unmatched qualities next.

The Descriptive Aspect of God

Just what is it that makes God, GOD? What is it that distinguishes him apart from the rest of creation as the one true God who is altogether different?

Fortunately, we are privileged to not only have God clearly tell us who he is through the written record in the Bible, but also to have him describe personal characteristics about himself. One of the best-known texts where we see this personal side of God is in Exodus 3. This passage reveals three unrivaled attributes that sequester him from all else as uniquely God:

> Then Moses said to God, "If I come to the people of Israel and say to them, 'The God of your fathers has sent me to you,' and they ask me, 'What is his name?' what shall I say to them?" God said to Moses, *"I AM WHO I AM."* And he said, "Say this to the people of Israel, *'I AM* has sent me to you.'" God also said to Moses, "Say this to the people of Israel, 'The LORD, the God of your fathers, the God of Abraham, the God of Isaac, and the God of Jacob, has sent me to you.' This is my name *forever*, and thus I am to be remembered throughout all generations." (Exodus 3:13-15)

Throughout the Bible we read about God making himself known to his creation via use of a proper name with titles or roles attached. These titles are used to reveal distinctive characteristics that reside in him. God is identified in Scripture by names such as: The Strong One; The Most High God; God our Healer; God Almighty; God our Provider; and the Everlasting God; to mention just a few.

That is not unlike someone today who would choose to distinctly identify himself via an official prefix, his surname, and degree earned . . . like Mr. Bunyan, A.S.E. (A.S.E. = Axe Slinger Extraordinaire). With an official prefix attached to the surname along with the post-nominal letters, we know this person is a male, has an identifiable family name, and is connected with the logging industry in some fashion.

We apply this same identity technique when we hear the title "Mr. President" used to officially address the President of the United States. Using an official prefix with a surname or a title and perhaps a degree or role attached to the name, such as M.D. or PhD., tells us something significant about a person.

But when Mr. Bunyan declares to us: "Please, call me Paul," or Mr. President replies: "You may call me Ronald," there is a personal aspect of the person that is now unveiled. It opens another dimension for understanding. By revealing his personal name voluntarily, he is extending an invitation for connection, for personal acquaintance, and perhaps a relationship.

While this naming convention illustration still falls far short of a proper description of God, it can give us an idea by comparison of what God is intending to do here.

In Moses' initial exposure to the burning bush experience where he meets his Maker (Exodus 3), God identifies himself as: "*I AM WHO I AM*," and instructs Moses to disclose to those who will listen to him that: "*I AM* has sent me to you." What we have here is God introducing himself to Moses by personal name.

The name *I AM* is normally translated Yahweh (from the four Hebrew consonants - *YHWH*) or LORD (all caps) as seen in most English translations of the Bible. Over the centuries linguistic scholars have found it difficult to definitively describe what God's personal name actually means. The idea 'to be' or 'to exist' seems to come close to its contextual definition, but the ramifications of its meaning is really quite expansive. All this helps in our understanding of God's description of himself. God desires to be properly acknowledged by his creation. God wants each of us to recognize his rightful place in our lives.

It is in this watershed moment for Moses that God introduces to all who would have ears to hear, three formative certainties regarding his nature.

First, God is Telling Us That He is Eternal

God describes himself as having no beginning and no end. He informs Moses, via his personal name, that he is the One who has always existed.

In our own finiteness it is unattainable to envision God having always been there. Nevertheless, God confidently assures us, through the identity of his own name, that he never had a moment of beginning. His name also informs us that he will never cease to be. He describes himself as being in existence for all eternity—in both directions. There never has, nor will there ever be, a time when there is not God.

Abraham planted a tamarisk tree in Beersheba and called there on the name of the LORD, *the Everlasting God*. (Genesis 21:33)

"See now that I, even I, am he, and there is no god beside me; I kill and I make alive; I wound and I heal; and there is none that can deliver out of my hand. For I lift up my hand to heaven and swear, *As I live forever,*" (Deuteronomy 32:39-40)

THERE IS NO OTHER

The eternal God is your dwelling place, and underneath are *the everlasting arms.* (Deuteronomy 33:27a)

Before the mountains were brought forth, or ever you had formed the earth and the world, *from everlasting to everlasting you are God.* (Psalm 90:2)

And the angel whom I saw standing on the sea and on the land raised his right hand to heaven and swore by *him who lives forever and ever,* who created heaven and what is in it, the earth and what is in it, and the sea and what is in it, that there would be no more delay, but that in the days of the trumpet call to be sounded by the seventh angel, the mystery of God would be fulfilled, just as he announced to his servants the prophets. (Revelation 10:5-7)

Secondly, God is Telling Us That He is Self-existing

God is completely independent of all things outside of himself. This, too, like the eternality of God, cannot be fully sensed in the midst of our own dependence upon external elements such as air, water, and food, for our existence.

God describes himself as self-existing and self-sustaining. No other being possesses that ability. Practically speaking, this means that God is not obliged for his existence. He resides in himself. Though God is the cause of all things, the creator of all things, and the sustainer of all things, there is no cause affixed to God's own existence. There is no other creator that God is indebted to. God truly is all in all in himself.

For as *the Father has life in himself,* so he has granted the Son also to have life in himself. (John 5:26)

So Paul, standing in the midst of the Areopagus, said: "Men of Athens, I perceive that in every way you are very religious. For as I passed along and observed the objects of your worship, I found also an altar with this inscription, To the unknown god.' What therefore you worship as unknown, this I proclaim to you. The God who made the world and everything in it, being Lord of heaven and earth, *does not live in temples made by man, nor is he served by human hands, as though he needed anything, since he himself gives to all mankind life and breath and everything."* (Acts 17:22-25)

Thirdly, God is Telling Us That He is Unchangeable

The name Yahweh also exposes us to the reality of the unalterable aspect of God. God exists outside of the laws of the creation regarding life and death, to which we humans are confined—at least for the moment. God's own declaration in Malachi reiterates this: "For I the LORD do not change" (3:6a). God is telling us in the name *I AM* that he is the same as he has always been, steadfast and consistent. God does not change nor is he subject to change. That can produce a wonderful security for us—we who find ourselves in a constant state of flux and persistent vacillation. Mankind changes. Creation changes. God does not.

It is also important to recognize that while God tells us he is unchanging, he is not static. God often will break through the drawn curtain of our own existence to make himself known, revealing his presence, demonstrating that he is living, personal, and actively at work in, through and on behalf of his people.

God is not man, that he should lie, or a son of man, that he should change his mind. Has he said, and will he not do it? Or has he spoken, and will he not fulfill it? (Numbers 23:19)

THERE IS NO OTHER

And also the *Glory of Israel will not lie or have regret*, for he is not a man, that he should have regret. (1 Samuel 15:29)

Every good gift and every perfect gift is from above, coming down from *the Father of lights with whom there is no variation or shadow due to change.* (James 1:17)

Admittedly, these descriptions only begin to scratch the surface of this great God of ours. It is a marvelous thing that he has chosen to reveal himself, which can produce an authentic awareness of our relationship to him. And while our ability to comprehend God is profoundly limited, still, we are invited to investigate, pursue, ponder, and eventually yield. He knows that if our drawing near to him is open, honest, and sincere, we will surely find him.

The Comparative Aspect of God

God is not afraid of comparison. God is not fearful with hat in hand, dreading that if we step onto the path of a passionate pursuit of our Creator that we will discover something other than what he has revealed to us. In fact, there are times in the Bible when God seems to invite comparison. Have a look at these verses:

Who is like you, O LORD, among the gods? *Who is like you*, majestic in holiness, awesome in glorious deeds, doing wonders? (Exodus 15:11)

There is *none holy like the LORD*; there is none besides you; there is no rock like our God. (1 Sam. 2:2)

You have multiplied, O LORD my God, your wondrous deeds and your thoughts toward us; *none can compare* with you! I will proclaim and tell of them, yet they are more than can be told. (Psalm 40:5)

For who in the skies *can be compared* to the LORD? Who among the heavenly beings is *like the LORD*? (Psalm 89:6)

"*To whom then will you compare me*, that I should be like him?" says the Holy One. (Isaiah 40:25)

"To whom *will you liken me* and *make me equal*, and *compare me*, that we may be alike?" (Isaiah 46:5)

It is rather obvious from these declarations that God is speaking to his creation in rhetorical fashion; none can compare. But even in God's own created world where he demonstrates over and over that there is no other god, there is still the temptation to construct and invoke our own fanciful idea of a god who can compete. This propensity is a result of our spiritual fallout, which will be addressed in a later chapter. For the moment, God has been declared as the incomparable Creator of all things. Practically speaking, this means that he is your Creator too! God has declared it is so.

The Collaborative Aspect of God

Before this chapter concludes there is another aspect of God that should be addressed. He has told us in his Word that he is a triune God—a Trinity; there are three who are equally one: Father, Son, and Holy Spirit.

There are many wonderful resources available for discussing the biblical doctrine of the Trinity at length. In this book, the Trinity will be touched upon periodically, revealing the scriptural truth and necessity of a triune God, but not in doctrinal detail.

Suffice it to say, throughout the Bible you will find the truth of the Trinity plainly laid out: God the Father is God; Jesus the Son is God; the Holy Spirit is God; all described as distinct, and at the same time, defined as one God. That said, you will not discover a verse in the Bible that says: "This is what the Trinity looks like and how the three work together as one." In fact, you won't find the word 'Trinity' anywhere in the Bible.

When studying any doctrine, it is important to remember that God has given us the Bible in complete book form. Therefore, we should never try to understand Scripture through a Yellow Pages® approach. While verse reference points can be of great help to us in locating segments of Scripture, God has spoken to us in complete thoughts through narratives, letters, prophecies, poetry, songs, etc., all weaving an intricate tapestry of God's extraordinary account of how it all began, how it all continues, and how it will all end.

One cannot deny that certain aspects of God's triune nature remain a mystery; even within the story he has told us. We must keep in mind that while God tells us the truth; he does not exhaust the truth. God tells us enough for faith, but he doesn't reveal so much as to remove our need for him.

When speaking of the Trinity, one must exercise caution when describing its meaning. Some have tried to simplify its definition by using the concept of three roles played by the same God, similar to a man who takes on the role of husband, father, and son, depending upon the situation. This illustration dilutes the truth of three distinct persons who are all equally God all the time.

Others have compared the Trinity's essence to water, ice, and steam, all different, yet being made up of the same substance. The problem with this is that each expression is wholly dependent upon their environment (exposure to hot or cold) to determine what they will become. We cannot overlook this truth; God is self-existent and self-sustaining, in need of nothing other than himself to be a Trinity. Truth be told, there are certain expressions of the uncreated God that cannot be explained using created elements. Remember, this is a journey of faith.

This we do know from Scripture; the triune God is eternal and unchangeable. The Son and the Spirit have been there with the Father from the beginning, all equally God. The Father, the Son, and the Holy Spirit work in perfect concert in order to bring to completion their predetermined blueprint for all of creation.

Here are a few truths from Scripture for further study. In order to capture the intent of what God is saying, it is always best to read verses in their context, both of the surrounding sentences as well as paragraphs and sections.

• There is one God — Deuteronomy 4:35, 39; 32:39; Isaiah 37:20; 43:10; 44:6; 45:5, 14, 21-22; 46:9; Jeremiah 10:10; John 5:44; Romans 3:30; 16:27; Galatians. 3:20; Ephesians 4:6; 1 Timothy 1:17; 2:5; James 2:19; 1 John 5:20; Jude 1:25

• There is Plurality and Distinction in the Trinity — Genesis 1:1, 26; 3:22; 11:7; Matthew 3:16-17; 28:19-20; 2 Corinthians 13:14

• The Father is God — 1 Corinthians 8:6; 2 Corinthians 1:3; Ephesians 1:3

- The Son is God — Isaiah 9:6; John 1:1-3, 14, 18; 10:30; 14:23; 15:26; 20:28; Romans 8:9; 9:5; Colossians 2:9; Titus 2:13; Hebrews 1:8; 2 Peter 1:1; Revelation 4:11

- The Holy Spirit is God — Genesis 1:2; Psalm 104:30; Matthew 1:18, 20; Luke 1:35; Acts 5:3-4; Romans 1:4; 8:11; 1 Corinthians 3:16; 2 Corinthians 3:17-18; Hebrews 3:7

Recalibration

God wants to be encountered. He wishes to be known. He instructs each of us to have faith, believing that he is the only true God. Yes, even to this very day, the eternal, self-existent, and unchangeable God continues to extend an invitation to every man and woman; seek for him and draw near with the assurance that he is a rewarder of anyone who finds him. Personally discovering the one true God—the all-powerful Creator—the generous Rewarder—now what could be a better find than that?

Draw near to God, and he will draw near to you. (James 4:8a)

Discussion Questions

1. Why is belief in the existence of God important?

2. What other gods are in competition with the God of the Bible?

3. What makes the God of the Bible different from all other gods?

4. How might one explain to another the truth of the Trinity?

5. Why is it a worthy effort to pursue God?

Praise him, sun and moon, praise him, all you shining stars!
Psalm 148

Moonrise in the Superstition Wilderness - Arizona

The heavens are yours; the earth also is yours; the world
and all that is in it, you have founded them.

Psalm 89

2

CONSIDER THE UNIVERSE . . .

nothing has been left to chance

True to form, our culture continues to generate a tremendous amount of speculation with regard to the existence of the physical universe. Listening carefully, we discover that most conjecture will, as a rule, land under one of these two categories: How did it all originally start? What path or paths have gotten us to where we are today? It is apparent that the mysteries that surround our beginnings continue to hold sway over varied fields of study: e.g., the religious, spiritual, philosophical and scientific disciplines.

Like a person standing in line at Starbucks®, we see before us a huge menu of choices being offered with regard to the creation story. This book is not intended to provide a comparison of opposing ideas being purported today. No, only one item is being selected off the menu; we are going to revisit God's own descriptive account of how the world was created as found in the book of Genesis.

When speaking of creation in this chapter, the focus will be upon both the universe as a whole and the universe in detail—both the seen and unseen aspects of life.

The Bible asserts that not only must we believe in the existence of God, but that we must also possess a faith that all things come from God. Hebrews 11—regarded by many as the 'Hall of Faith' section of the Bible—provides us a concise description of how faith is essential to connecting our lives with the story: "By faith we understand that *the universe was created by the word of God, so that what is seen was not made out of things that are visible*" (Hebrews 11:3).

The writer tells us *what* was created: the *entire universe*. He then describes for us *how* it was accomplished: by *God's speaking something into existence out of nothing*.

Despite those in our culture who will continue asserting that natural creation is possible apart from a supernatural God, creation 'out of nothing' will always remain God's intellectual property. We will never be invited into God's kitchen to copy his original recipes; but not to be discouraged, we have been extended an offer to take our place in the family room where we may enjoy the aroma, be blessed with some great conversation, and marvel at the view. Pretty incredible stuff!

The mere belief in the truth of supernatural creation is indeed a great opportunity for the expression of our faith, but there's much more to the story. Not only did God speak things into existence, we are also told in Scripture that God then began to sustain creation miraculously: "He is the radiance of the glory of God and the exact imprint of his nature, and *he upholds the universe by the word of his power*" (Hebrews 1:3a).

The following passages also affirm this truth:

As it is written, "I have made you the father of many nations"—in the presence of the God in whom he believed, who gives life to the dead and *calls into existence the things* that do not exist. (Romans 4:17)

Yet for us there is one God, the Father, from whom are all things and *for whom we exist*, and one Lord, Jesus Christ, through whom are all things and *through whom we exist*. (1 Corinthians 8:6)

For it was fitting that he, *for whom and by whom all things exist*, in bringing many sons to glory, should make the founder of their salvation perfect through suffering. (Hebrews 2:10)

We owe our existence to God's initial desire to create. In addition, we can be eternally grateful for God's tirelessly supplying and sustaining everything we need in order to live. There is never a moment in God's schedule where we will find him depleted, used up, or out of energy. God never has too much on his plate. Listen to the prophet Isaiah: "Have you not known? Have you not heard? The LORD is the everlasting God, the Creator of the ends of the earth. *He does not faint or grow weary*; his understanding is unsearchable" (Isaiah 40:28). That, my friend, is an awesome God!

God the Creator

So what particulars does God want us to know about himself with regard to creation? First, and most notable, God expects us to accept by faith this simple statement: "*In the beginning, God created the heavens and the earth*" (Genesis 1:1). This verse is paramount to one's pursuit of God. If you refuse to believe the accuracy of this proclamation, nothing else that God says or does will make sense.

While Genesis 1:1 is simple to read and easy to memorize, the verse is chock-full of truth and insight that can help us begin to properly understand our surroundings.

God wants us to know this truth: an infinite, all-powerful, self-existent God has created the universe in which we dwell. This heaven and earth, God declares, had a beginning—but it was so much more than just a big bang.

In this chapter we are going to touch on three key aspects of God's creative process: The Power of God's Spoken Word, The Revelation of Divine Order, and the Miracle of God's Sustenance of Life. Again, this is not a lesson in creation—it is an attempt to convey what God wants known about himself.

The Power of God's Spoken Word

The Bible is unquestionably clear when it comes to describing the creative verbal powers of God. The Hebrew word in Genesis for God's creative process is *bara,* which is defined as God's act of creating by divine fiat—a Latin term meaning: "Let there be." The essence of the word assigns origins to God's powerfully creating all things through speaking. The Bible's intention is to publicize the truth that God created the entire universe out of absolutely nothing, completely void of any substance whatsoever, including light and energy. The biblical story of creation reveals the self-existent power of God.

Since no one was there in the beginning but God, and since no one can return to the original event, it is a requisite that faith in God be the primary component in our approach to the creation of the physical universe. Do not overlook this fact; every other account of creation that would exclude God from the story is also a faith effort. It doesn't matter which academic or scientific celebrity declares it; it doesn't matter how loud and authoritative they become; it doesn't matter in how many textbooks it appears; still, the creation account of the world is a faith journey for all.

A person's understanding of creation is *always* based upon certain presuppositions. Does God exist? Could creation happen the way we read it in Genesis 1? Did the one who recorded the story as told in Genesis 1 get the facts right? Is the Genesis account of creation reliable when compared to the world as we see it today?

Your answers to those questions: a 'yes', 'no', 'maybe', or 'I don't know', are your presuppositions from which you draw your life conclusions about God and the universe. If you don't believe God exists in the first place, then you won't look for God in a book like the Bible, in the world around you, nor in your own life. Note it is not that God is hiding from you; it is that you simply refuse to recognize that God is there. Romans 1 describes the person who says 'there is no God' as one who is attempting to suppress the truth. It is like a person sitting on an overstuffed suitcase straining with all his or her might to click it shut, but without success.

On the other hand, if you do believe God exists, then you will look for the story of God in a book like the Bible, in the world around you, and in your own life. What you observe in the world—while often mysterious and complex—will fit your presupposition that God is there, God is active, and that God is personal. The one who believes sees the Creator's fingerprints upon the pages they read, upon the world in which they live, and upon their own life.

That is why it is imperative that anyone who would seek for God must exercise his or her faith, believing that he exists. Your own presupposition about what you believe to be true or false will have a direct effect on how you choose to live your life.

We must not forget that we live in a hostile world; the Christian belief in God is being tenaciously suppressed, attacked, and discredited. We are witnessing a culture act out its confidence that there is no Creator. Still, one cannot escape the fact that people throughout the world hold to some sort of creation story or creation account, whether it be God, chaos, or evolution. Again, their presuppositions will be the filter through which their points of resistance will be determined, and what they will choose to believe.

A follower of God believes that God has revealed himself, is truthful, and does not lie. For the Christian, this provides the foundation upon which to build his or her life and worldview. One must also allow for the supernatural if we would make sense of creation. Listen to what the Biblical record says about the creative power of God's spoken word:

They will say, "Where is the promise of his coming? For ever since the fathers fell asleep, all things are continuing as they were from the beginning of creation." For they deliberately overlook this fact, that *the heavens existed long ago, and the earth was formed out of water and through water by the word of God,* (2 Peter 3:4-5)

By the word of the LORD the heavens were made, and by the breath of his mouth all their host. He gathers the waters of the sea as a heap; he puts the deeps in storehouses. Let all the earth fear the LORD; let all the inhabitants of the world stand in awe of him! *For he spoke, and it came to be; he commanded, and it stood firm.* (Psalm 33:6-9)

"So *shall my word be that goes out from my mouth; it shall not return to me empty, but it shall accomplish that which I purpose*, and shall succeed in the thing for which I sent it." (Isaiah 55:11)

The story of God has been proven to be true and reliable, having supernaturally withstood repeated attacks throughout the millennia, fending off accusation after accusation from those who insist that we must relegate God to myth and therefore render the creation account as legend. If God is not who he says he is, then we need to stop what we are doing and get about the business of self-seeking pleasure: "Let us eat and drink, for tomorrow we die" (1 Corinthians 15:32b).

For the Christian, that is impossible. There are just too many observable facts in creation to deny the reality that there was and is a divine Designer behind it all. This is not a closed or chaotic world system as the nature television shows would have us assume. God is not an evolutionary god. God has not put anything on an evolutionary path. God created out of divine fiat, not divine evolution. God has truly supernaturally created all things. As stated earlier, if we refuse to accept the accuracy of Genesis 1:1, nothing else will make sense; nothing else will matter. Conversely, if Genesis 1:1 is an accurate statement, we have every good reason to believe the rest of the story.

The Revelation of Divine Order

Let us now examine the creation event. A basic feature readers will note in this account is that there is order to creation. Here is the actual creation record as found in chapter one of Genesis:

Introductory Declaration: v. 1: In the beginning, God created the heavens and the earth.

Setting the Stage: v. 2: The earth was without form and void, and darkness was over the face of the deep. And the Spirit of God was hovering over the face of the waters.

Day One: vv. 3-5: 3And God said, "*Let there be* light," and there was light. 4And God saw that the light was good. And God separated the light from the darkness. 5God called the light Day, and the darkness he called Night. *And there was evening and there was morning, the first day.*

Day Two: vv. 6-8: 6And God said, "*Let there be* an expanse in the midst of the waters, and let it separate the waters from the waters." 7And God made the expanse and separated the waters that were under the expanse from the waters that were above the expanse. And it was so. 8And God called the expanse Heaven. *And there was evening and there was morning, the second day.*

Day Three: vv. 9-13: 9And God said, "*Let the waters under the heavens be gathered together into one place, and let the dry land appear.*" And it was so. 10God called the dry land Earth, and the waters that were gathered together he called Seas. And God saw that it was good. 11And God said, "Let the earth sprout vegetation, plants yielding seed, and fruit trees bearing fruit in which is their seed, each according to its kind, on the earth." And it was so. 12The earth brought forth vegetation, plants yielding seed according to their own kinds, and trees bearing fruit in which is their seed, each according to its kind. And God saw that it was good. [13]*And there was evening and there was morning, the third day.*

Day Four: vv. 14-19: [14]And God said, *"Let there be* lights in the expanse of the heavens to separate the day from the night. And let them be for signs and for seasons, and for days and years, [15]and let them be lights in the expanse of the heavens to give light upon the earth." And it was so. [16]And God made the two great lights—the greater light to rule the day and the lesser light to rule the night—and the stars. [17]And God set them in the expanse of the heavens to give light on the earth, [18]to rule over the day and over the night, and to separate the light from the darkness. And God saw that it was good. [19]*And there was evening and there was morning, the fourth day.*

Day Five: vv. 20-23: [20]And God said, *"Let the waters swarm with swarms of living creatures, and let birds fly above the earth across the expanse of the heavens."* [21]So God created the great sea creatures and every living creature that moves, with which the waters swarm, according to their kinds, and every winged bird according to its kind. And God saw that it was good. [22]And God blessed them, saying, "Be fruitful and multiply and fill the waters in the seas, and let birds multiply on the earth." [23]*And there was evening and there was morning, the fifth day.*

Day Six: vv. 24-31: [24]And God said, *"Let the earth bring forth living creatures according to their kinds—livestock and creeping things and beasts of the earth according to their kinds."* And it was so. [25]And God made the beasts of the earth according to their kinds and the livestock according to their kinds, and everything that creeps on the ground according to its kind. And God saw that it was good. [26]Then God said, "Let us make man in our image, after our likeness. And let them have dominion over the fish of the sea and over the birds of the heavens and over the livestock and over all the earth and over every creeping thing that creeps on the earth." [27]So God created man in his own image, in the image of God he created him; male and female he created them. [28]And God blessed them. And God said to them, "Be fruitful and multiply and fill the earth and subdue it and have dominion over the fish of the sea and over the birds of the heavens and over every living thing that moves on the earth." [29]And God said, "Behold, I have given you every plant yielding seed that is on the face of all the earth, and every tree with seed in its fruit. You shall have them for food. [30]And to every beast of the earth and to every bird of the heavens and to everything that creeps on the earth, everything that has the breath of life, I have given every green plant for food." And it was so. [31]And God saw everything that he had made, and behold, it was very good. *And there was evening and there was morning, the sixth day.*

And from chapter two:

Day Seven: vv. 1-3: [1]Thus the heavens and the earth were finished, and all the host of them. [2]And on the seventh day God finished his work that he had done, and he rested on the seventh day from all his work that he had done. [3]So God blessed the seventh day and made it holy, because on it God rested from all his work that he had done in creation.

This is the initial account from God's story on how all things have come into existence. While the description is incredible itself, there are several prominent particulars to note:

Was Each Day an Actual 24 Hour Day? – We can reply here with a "yes" based upon the *presupposition* that God exists, that God could do it, and he seems to indicate in the actual account that he did. The text of Genesis 1 itself provides sufficient evidence to suggest that the author intended to place the creation account in the framework of seven 24-hour days. Here are a few indicators to consider:

1. There is morning and evening terminology used in the account.
2. Genesis 1:5 define a day as a period of light and darkness.
3. The Hebrew word *yom* "day" is used in this text 14 times.
4. The word *yom* "day" is numerically qualified for us seven times, day one, day two, etc.
5. Normally when the word *yom* "day" is used with a numeric qualifier, it is intended to be understood in literal sense and not in a non-literal sense.

Does Kind and Species Mean the Same Thing? – It is clear that the Scriptures declare that God created each animal, bird, and fish, after their own kind. In recent years man has chosen to introduce his own system of micro classification of the species, thereby attempting to force the notion—without God in the mix—that all species must be permitted, by natural selection (the will to survive), to cross over and breed with other species, thus mutating biologically; resulting in new advanced species for classification.

It is easily observable that God's classification of *kind* in Genesis has a broader intent in mind than mankind's determination to classify in detail. It is also noteworthy to see some modern scientists returning to a simpler, broader definition of species, recognizing the existence of distinct and unalterable boundaries between kinds as described in the biblical creation account. While volumes have been penned in this area of study, we are keeping with our premise: What does God want us to know about himself?

God declares to us that he created all things, which includes the gene pool of the species. And while God did not create in an evolutionary fashion, there remains room for expansion within each particular kind. For instance, there is no biblical conflict with the continued development of various breeds, of say, dogs, *within their own kind.* Did God create the German Shepherd, Chihuahua, and Toy Poodle all on the sixth day? It is doubtful. But to be true to Scripture, God created each kind as distinct and particular—dogs will never become cats—cats will never become mice—mice will never become fleas—but to be sure, all have been created for his purpose and glory—yes, even fleas.

While we have the record in our hands, there is still much we do not know about the creation event because God has chosen not to make it known. We cannot forget that this is a faith journey; God is telling us his story and he confidently asserts that he does not lie.

Next, let's look at the same creation account, but from a different perspective:

Creation Order – Genesis 1

Day 1: Light and Darkness (vv. 3-5)	Day 4: Sun/Moon (vv. 14-19)
Day 2: Sky/Water (vv. 6-8)	Day 5: Birds/Fish (vv. 20-23)
Day 3: Land/Vegetation (vv. 9-13)	Day 6: Animals/Man (vv. 24-31)

Do you notice anything interesting about the divine order here? In case you don't see it, it appears that God used the first three days to create three particular environments; shells so to speak, and then proceeded on days 4-6 to populate their respective settings. Even the methodology of creation reveals order and structure.

Life is neither chaotic nor haphazard. God has always worked moving forward, and will continue doing so, using order and intent as he turns his blueprint for all the ages into reality. History is not circular, as some would teach. While we may repeat our own mistakes with some regularity, God is in fact moving history in linear fashion toward the horizon of completion, and he has invited us to be a part.

The Miracle of God's Sustenance of Life

Scientists have spent entire careers attempting to unravel and expose the secret behind the existence of all things: How is existence actually accomplished? Who flips the 'on' switch to start life and growth? Who keeps it going? What force is generating it? And why do things run out of energy and die?

Admittedly, all agree that living organisms have a place of beginning; they grow and mature and then eventually break down, die, and decay. But despite all their experimental efforts, scientists have been unable to unravel the initial cause for controlled creation and order—how the actual time of activation is determined, and thus how the activation process commences. In other words, who gives the "Create!" command? Who gives the "Grow!" command?

Without question, many detailed aspects of creation can be observed, but any attempt to produce a usable and repeatable 'on switch' for mankind's god-like creation apparatus will predictably result in failure. It is contended that man's pursuit of decrypting divine creative formulations apart from God will remain forever futile. For to understand the creation order properly, one must acknowledge the existence of both a divine genetic code embedded in all living things, and a supernatural 'God-switch' that alone activates the code. God, the Bible declares, is the Giver of all life, as we know it (1 Timothy 6:13).

Scientists have given these genetic processes a name: *Teleonomy*. Teleonomy, defined in rather simplistic fashion, is genetic code—resident in all living things—specifically reserved for the purpose of capturing and using energy for order and direction, and for growth and complexity. Evolutionists believe that the existence of teleonomy requires no external intervention. A living thing doesn't depend upon a designer to have the actual genetic code placed within, nor is there a need for a supernatural activator. They assert that life can create, develop, and maintain its own genetic code and that a living organism can activate teleonomy when deemed necessary for its survival—commanding itself to begin capturing energy in order to advance organization, complexity, and growth. Again, for the evolutionist, this whole process has come about through countless chance happenings over an unimaginable period of time.

How is teleonomy used? Let's use the acorn as an example. An acorn's inherent teleonomy or specific genetic code will wait patiently until it is intentionally activated at a precisely given moment by 'something'—for the Christian this 'something' is God—which in turn instructs an acorn to use its stored code to become an oak tree. In the same manner, it is the use of this unseen command of God—turning on the internal genetic code—that will intentionally tell a bulb at a precise moment that it is time to become a tulip. Interestingly, teleonomy is completely absent in non-living matter. For the person who believes that God created all things, one would expect this since non-living matter has no intention.

When scientists define and explain teleonomy, are they unwittingly identifying God's supernatural method of both causing and sustaining the existence of all living things? Is this an area of scientific exploration intended to perpetually frustrate man's quest to capture the secrets of the origin of life apart from God's revelation? Will man accept the reality that while he may examine the results of the creation of life, he is not permitted to activate life on his own, because it is God who alone keeps his finger on the switch?

God is at work in living things because God is the living God. We must believe he exists and we must have faith that what we read and experience is true because God has told us so. He has set into place when things are to be, to come to life, and grow; and he has set into place when things should not be, but instead, break down, die, and decay.

Recalibration

Our knowledge is currently set to double every two and a half years. Knowing this, we must resist the temptation to carry this ever-increasing creative genius God has given us into the realm of the unseen world, always trying to unravel the code of the divine Creator. Yes, the creation questions will continue to be asked. God predicted they would. The writer of Ecclesiastes puts it this way: "He has made everything beautiful in its time. Also, he has put eternity into man's heart, yet so that *he cannot find out what God has done from the beginning to the end*" (3:11). Any attempt to actually decipher and replicate God's creative handiwork will serve only to expose a man or woman's own finite limitations.

While there is a whole lot more to the story of creation itself, the primary focus here is what God wants us to know about himself as the Creator. Most significantly, God desires that each and every one of us *know him personally,* and not just know things about him. He is fully aware that we cannot perceive everything about creation, but he does assure us he has revealed sufficient evidence for personal faith in him. Remember, this is the creator God who is elaborately detailed in all he does, highly organized in all his actions, and extremely generous with all he owns. He is the God who can be known intimately by his creation; and he is the God who dwells in the secret places of incomprehensible mystery. He is the great and mighty God!

To conclude, there always comes a certain juncture in the whole discussion of creation where we are encouraged to just step back and marvel at his handiwork rather than concentrate on all the formulas, equations, and possibilities. It is in those moments of contemplation that God seems most pleased.

When I look at your heavens, the work of your fingers, the moon and the stars, which you have set in place, what is man that you are mindful of him, and the son of man that you care for him? Yet you have made him a little lower than the heavenly beings and crowned him with glory and honor. (Psalm 8:3-5)

Discussion Questions

1. Why is faith in God necessary with regard to creation?

2. How does one's own presuppositions affect their worldview?

3. Why is Genesis 1:1 such an important starting point with God?

4. Why is God's power to sustain essential to life?

5. Why do people struggle with the truth about creation?

The Gift of Life - Tempe, Arizona

The LORD God formed the man of dust from the ground
and breathed into his nostrils the breath of life.

Genesis 2

3

GIVER OF LIFE . . .

male and female he created them

God has openly and unapologetically taken ownership of the origins of mankind. Genesis 1 says:

> Then God said, *"Let us make man in our image, after our likeness. And let them have dominion over the fish of the sea and over the birds of the heavens and over the livestock and over all the earth and over every creeping thing that creeps on the earth." So God created man in his own image*, in the image of God he created him; male and female he created them. (Genesis 1:26-27)

It was God who created Adam and Eve, our first parents, as his crowning creative achievement. This is our shared quality with everything animal, vegetable, and mineral; God has created all things—but this is where the commonality with the rest of creation also ends.

While all creation is finite and owes its existence to the Creator, there is something quite unique that sets man apart from the rest of what God has made. Genesis tells us that we have been created in the image of God. God reveals that we were formed—both man and woman—in his likeness. Here you have the first indication in the Bible that man is unparalleled in the order of God's creation. He is unique in the responsibilities he's been given, in the area of relationships he will develop, and in the realm of his own personal makeup. Listen to the Psalmist reflect upon the miracle of his own existence:

> I praise you, for *I am fearfully and wonderfully made.* Wonderful are your works; my soul knows it very well. My frame was not hidden from you, when *I was being made in secret,* intricately woven in the depths of the earth. *Your eyes saw my unformed substance;* in your book were written, every one of them, the days that were formed for me, when as yet there was none of them. (Psalm 139:14-16)

Contrary to the popular belief today—that man started out as some sort of primeval creature sitting in a cold, damp cave, forced to enter into life's evolutionary struggle in order to get to where he is—God tells us that he created the first man and woman in complete perfection; fully functional upright adults equipped with an unbiased mind to know what is true, and an unprejudiced heart to sense what is right.

When addressing the biblical truth that mankind is much more than just an advanced species of animal—a mammal to be specific, merely created by the process of random chance happenings—but is instead, a uniquely fashioned living and breathing miracle of God's handiwork, we must be prepared to provide a satisfactory reply to those who would seem convinced otherwise. If one is serious about speaking what is true, he or she needs to be prepared to offer sincere and straightforward answers to the two most common questions asked with regard to God being our creator:

1. Is there any discernable evidence residing in us that would demonstrate that we have been created in the image of God?

2. Is there any discernable evidence residing in us that would affirm that we are distinct from the animal world?

One can answer both questions with a definitive 'yes' by way of simple reflection on five particular attributes evident in each of us—traits that have been supernaturally imparted to us by God—characteristics which distinctly set us apart from the rest of the created world, thus establishing our being uniquely crafted in his image.

First: The Attribute of Personality

Let's start with the most basic trait we exhibit as bearers of the image of God. We are *personal* just as God is personal; therefore, we are not impersonal animalistic creatures driven by instinct in a machine-like fashion. We inherently know this to be true—that there is more to us than mere natural causes of survival, but in spite of the demonstration of our imparted 'personalness,' mankind seems determined to go to great lengths to invalidate our own consciousness of it. Still, it is this personal awareness of self and of our Creator that serves to confirm that our rudiments do not reside in the animal kingdom.

To take this a step further, it is because we are personal beings we can know both the emotion and the reality of love. The love we possess can be personally experienced, as well as voluntarily extended to others. Love fulfills the felt need for intimacy that we all crave. Our ability and desire to love is a divine signpost that affirms our created personal nature. We are made for relationship with God and we are made for relationship with each other. The love we offer and receive goes far beyond just the physical and psychological need for procreation in order to maintain the species. The personality we have been given demands intimacy because we are personal beings.

We are privileged to preview the origins of this personal nature we have received from God by way of his own creative command as recorded in Genesis 1. God, speaking, uses the plural: "Let us make man" (v. 26a). This text reveals God in intimate conversation within himself. This is our first exposure to the 'personal' aspect of the triune God, or what is known as the Trinity (see the Collaborative Aspect of God in chapter one). It is because this triune God—who is personal and dwells in the atmosphere of perfect love—decided to create each of one of us in his likeness that we find ourselves equipped with a wide range of emotions and capable of true feelings. We are not soulless creatures merely programmed to our surroundings. There is intention and purpose for our existence.

In view of the fact that the story God is telling is true about our being created in his likeness, we should therefore not think it strange or unusual to have been given a portion of the Creator's own personal nature. Thus, we see that personality resides in us all.

Second: The Attribute of Communication

We have been given verbalization and visual skills, divinely imparted, that permit us to communicate with our Creator in a personal way, as well as with others who are also created in his image. Through these abilities we are able to express our intentions, our thoughts, our dreams, our history, our understanding of God's truth, and our worship. The use of words permits us to articulate our musings, to dialogue, to identify, as well as it serves as our primary means by which we impart knowledge and wisdom to our own children. Words are the instrument by which we comprehend and understand each other.

Evolutionists assert that since it has been widely observed that animals possess both simple and complex communication methods, it is only proper to view man—the Homo sapien species naturally linked to the animal world—as merely possessing an advanced stage of communication abilities achieved through evolutionary processes.

A reply to this assertion is necessary: Since it is God who has created all things in the animal world as well, it should be of no surprise to observe God providing methods for animals to communicate to their own kind in order to find each other for pro-creation and identity purposes. But there is a vast difference between mankind's attentive interaction and the utilitarian exchange going on in the animal kingdom. Men and women are infinitely more expressive with their communication, which offers a far greater capacity for relationship, from a simple acquaintance to soulful intimacy. It is undeniable that the communication skills given to humanity transcend far beyond the mere need for identity and survival.

The Bible also provides the account of how all the world's languages came into being (Genesis 11). While it is unfortunate that mankind's insistence on ignoring God's rightful place in the creation necessitated the diversity of languages—yes, there was one original language—God took the extra step by providing the essential means by which we all can still interact with each other. God describes himself as being compassionate and longsuffering, even to those who continually deny him. Realistically, he could have made it much more difficult for all of us.

It is no coincidence that God used the power of his spoken word to call all things into existence. It is no coincidence that Jesus Christ himself is called the living Word or Logos (Greek word for word). It is no coincidence that God continues to communicate in a manner unique to humanity, unfolding a history for us while prophesying a redemptive future that will surely come to pass.

Third: The Attribute of Creativity

It is without question that humanity is highly imaginative, artistic, and inventive. This too, comes from God. Both the expression and appreciation of what our minds can envision models our Creator's creative nature. One can choose to express his or her creativity in useful ways, taking on a practical approach, and one can choose to express his or her creativity aesthetically, purely for the sake of beauty. The mere existence of creativity reveals the endowment of design that resides in us all, having been placed there by our Maker.

One way our creative attribute can be appreciated is in our passion to decorate—whether it is draping one's self in colorful clothes, or planting flowers—whether it be adorning a Christmas tree with ornaments and lights or dressing up our homes with furniture and wall-hangings—there is no mistaking that humanity loves to beautify. It is apparent that mankind's desire to express his or her creativity extends far beyond the evolutionist's utilitarian approach to life and serves as yet another example of our distinctiveness from the animal world.

Celebration of special moments such as birthdays, weddings, and holidays all depict creative moments wrought merely for the sake of enjoyment and recognition. Areas such as art, music, dance, film, theater, and literature illustrate our desire for expression—all affirming that creativity has been divinely given to every man and woman unlike any other creature. God has given man the gift to experience enjoyment and pleasure through his creativity.

God will, at times, take a man or woman's imparted creativity to a whole other level by giving a certain person or group a significant 'extra dose' of creativity in a particular area in order to achieve something very special. Listen to this account found in Exodus 35 as God was giving detailed instructions to Moses on how to construct the Tent in the Wilderness:

> Then Moses said to the people of Israel, "See, the LORD has called by name Bezalel the son of Uri, son of Hur, of the tribe of Judah; and *he has filled him with the Spirit of God, with skill, with intelligence, with knowledge, and with all craftsmanship, to devise artistic designs, to work in gold and silver and bronze, in cutting stones for setting, and in carving wood, for work in every skilled craft.* And he has inspired him to teach, both him and Oholiab the son of Ahisamach of the tribe of Dan. *He has filled them with skill to do every sort of work done by an engraver or by a designer or by an embroiderer in blue and purple and scarlet yarns and fine twined linen, or by a weaver—by any sort of workman or skilled designer."* (Exodus 35:30-35)

God is the sole source of our creativity. Whether the child prodigy, Mozart, or the gray-haired musician jamming in a band; whether the master painter, Rembrandt, or the finger-painter in day school; whether the seasoned wordsmith, Hemmingway, or a young mom attempting to put into words her true feelings; whether it be the visionary, Leonardo Da Vinci, or an elderly person building a scrapbook of memories . . . all owe their creative genius to their Creator.

Fourth: The Attribute of Morals

We observe from within our own conscience—supernaturally placed there by God—that there is in place a basic sense of right and wrong in the world. God has informed us that the knowledge of morality resides in each and every person.

> For when Gentiles, who do not have the law, by nature do what the law requires, they are a law to themselves, even though they do not have the law. *They show that the work of the law is written on their hearts, while their conscience also bears witness,* and their conflicting thoughts accuse or even excuse them. (Romans 2:14-15)

> For although *they knew God, they did not honor him as God* or give thanks to him, but they became futile in their thinking, and their foolish hearts were darkened. (Romans 1:21)

> So whoever knows the right thing to do and fails to do it, for him it is sin. (James 4:17)

Our desire to teach our children the difference between right and wrong demonstrates our basic understanding of the place of morals in this world. We need not teach our children to disobey, for they do this naturally—yet another example of the rebellion we inherited from our first parents. Because of our basic sense of morals, we insist that our children obey, following our rules and respecting authority. Instructing our children in basic morality is a responsibility that our heavenly Father has placed upon us as parents, so that children may know both right from wrong, and that they are accountable for their actions.

The sheer number of psychologists and psychiatrists practicing today sends a very clear message that our society possesses a tremendous sense of guilt, revealing yet again an innate sense of right and wrong. To counter this, our culture would have us live on mind-numbing medication or under the spell of endless gibberish in order to dispel any notion of personal guilt and accountability. But according to the Bible, pills and pep talks will never really produce the dulling affect we yearn for in order to feel less guilty about the wrong we have done.

Our cry for justice when we witness atrocities or hear of injustices through the media outlets is another example that reveals our inner-sense of knowing something about morality. Even the most sadistic and diabolical sociopath will still get upset at something he or she thinks is wrong, thus exposing his or her sense of morals, maladjusted though they may be.

The simple awareness of good and evil is yet another example of what sets us apart from the animal kingdom, affirming that we have been uniquely created in the image of God. If we are truly honest with ourselves, we know that any attempt to have an amoral approach to our existence is in fact, impossible. God has created us as moral beings to know right from wrong.

For God will bring every deed into judgment, with every secret thing, whether good or evil. (Ecclesiastes 12:14)

Fifth: The Attribute of Intelligence

God says in Genesis 2:

> Now out of the ground the LORD God had formed every beast of the field and every bird of the heavens and brought them to the man to see what he would call them. *And whatever the man called every living creature, that was its name. The man gave names to all livestock and to the birds of the heavens and to every beast of the field.* (Genesis 2:19-20a)

God gave Adam a mind. God gave Adam a mind to use. Notice Adam named every living creature. That's no small feat and merely demonstrates one aspect of the intellectual capacity God placed in Adam, which has been passed down to each one of us.

God has made us all exceptional thinkers, organizers, researchers, and builders. We are God's crowning design on so many levels, including the intellect. We demonstrate our intelligence through disciplines such as math, science, and philosophy. The computer automation of our culture in recent years reveals how we can cognitively pioneer into areas of technology previously unimagined. The discovery of cures for diseases and our ability to save a life through medical intervention validates how we can use our reasoning powers for good.

More Than a Chance Happening

If examined thoughtfully, one can see how all of these divinely imparted attributes complement one another. We long to use our minds because we are creative and imaginative people, and we crave to express ourselves. In that expression we look for ways to help others because we care.

We want to speak forth that we care because we, too, have a desire to hear that someone cares for us. We demonstrate our caring for others because down deep inside us, we know it is the right thing to do. Bottom-line, we can do nothing other than exhibit the attributes given to us by our Creator because that is who we are; that is our identity, tainted though those attributes may be with sin and our own self-interests.

Our lives affirm every single day that we bear the image of the one true God. Actually, the attributes we have been given are intended to serve an even a higher purpose in our lives: we have been given a mind so that we can *know* God; we have been given a heart so that we can *love* God; we have been given a will so that we can *obey* God. We are distinct from the rest of the created world. We have been uniquely created in the likeness of God.

Our First Parents

Let's get back to God's story and look at what else he considers important that we know about the creation of mankind:

These are the generations of the heavens and the earth when they were created, in the day that the LORD God made the earth and the heavens. When no bush of the field was yet in the land and no small plant of the field had yet sprung up— for the LORD God had not caused it to rain on the land, and there was no man to work the ground, and a mist was going up from the land and was watering the whole face of the ground— *then the LORD God formed the man of dust from the ground and breathed into his nostrils the breath of life, and the man became a living creature.* (Genesis 2:4-7)

The Bible declares that God created mankind supernaturally apart from any evolutionary process. He used the elements of this natural world (dust), but then proved that this created world was not just a naturalistically closed system by choosing to enter into it supernaturally, giving his own breath to Adam, who only then began to live.

This account makes sense when we witness the reality of the death and decay of mankind. The Bible declares: "For *dust you are* and to *dust you will return*" (Genesis 3:19b). One can't escape the fact that it is God who has decreed that death should touch us all. Now if we can trust the Bible to have properly recorded the truth of God's verdict concerning death, why do we find it difficult to trust that same God of the Bible to tell us the truth about life?

Note the description of the account continues:

> And the LORD God planted a garden in Eden, in the east, and there he put the man whom he had formed. And out of the ground *the LORD God made to spring up every tree that is pleasant to the sight and good for food.* (Genesis 2:8-9a)

Don't miss this weighty point: God created man and woman—whom he named Adam and Eve—both as mature adults who were able to immediately partake of the adult food (mature fruit) that God also had called into existence supernaturally.

Evolution's faith-based theory of the origin of life insists that we accept the premise that our existence started out in simple fashion as a single cell; that through eons of evolutionary processes and opportunity, life has become is what it is today, incredibly complex. Interestingly, this is wholly inconsistent with the observable *Second Law of*

Thermodynamics. This law, simply defined, is the universal principle that no living thing can perpetually maintain itself on its own. It is the fixed rule that all living things eventually run out of energy, break down, die, and decay, and it is in the process of decay that all living things move from complex to simple. The evolutionist has placed himself in direct contradiction to this constant, asserting that living things can naturally—through chance and time—progress *on their own* from simple to complex. According to their theory, a living organism does not necessarily have to fall prey to decay, but can instead, will itself—by some unique drive from within to survive—to perpetuate its own development into a new and improved species that had never previously existed.

God's story, in contrast to the evolutionary theory, is that man was supernaturally fashioned as a complete and whole person with no need for further advancement or development. God made man a fully functional, incredibly complex, and marvelously expressive human being. And yet, there was still something missing.

Let's look at God's account of the creation of woman:

> Then the LORD God said, "It is not good that the man should be alone; I will make him a helper fit for him." Now out of the ground the LORD God had formed every beast of the field and every bird of the heavens and brought them to the man to see what he would call them. And whatever the man called every living creature, that was its name. The man gave names to all livestock and to the birds of the heavens and to every beast of the field. *But for Adam there was not found a helper fit for him.* So the LORD God caused a deep sleep to fall upon the man, and while he slept took one of his ribs and closed up its place with flesh. And the rib that the LORD God had taken from the man he made into a

woman and brought her to the man. Then the man said, "This at last is bone of my bones and flesh of my flesh; she shall be called Woman, because she was taken out of Man." (Genesis 2:18-23)

It seems that God had a manifold purpose in letting Adam name all the animals:

• God permits Adam to perform this feat as his first responsibility in overseeing creation.

• We see that Adam is quite capable, proving he is supremely intelligent and possesses an extensive and highly creative vocabulary.

• By Adam's naming all the animals, Adam is to be seen as separate from the animal kingdom.

• God brought before Adam both male and female of each and every animal, thereby letting Adam experience a sense of incompleteness. While there seemed to be a 'Mr. & Mrs.' for all the other creatures, there was no 'Mrs. Adam.'

God wants us to trust this truth: that he is kind and compassionate and does not ignore our needs. Like Adam's felt need for companionship with Eve, God desires to complete what is incomplete in us, but he will always do it his way, and without fail, it will be what is best for us.

And I am sure of this, that he who began a good work in you will bring it to completion at the day of Jesus Christ. (Philippians 1:6)

And we know that for those who love God all things work together for good, for those who are called according to his purpose. (Romans 8:28)

Recalibration

From the first breath man took on the sixth day of the creation account up to this very moment in history, there has been a God-given three-fold mandate with regard to creation. God has instructed every man and woman to:

1. Reproduce - Fill the earth (Genesis 1:28a)
2. Reign - Have dominion over the earth (Genesis 1:28b)
3. Reflect – Mirror the image of God (Genesis 1:27)

To put it another way, the biblical mandate from Genesis 1 is to have children, responsibly rule over the earth, and live our lives in the likeness of our Creator, echoing his perfect ways in all we think, say, and do.

God has created all men and women miraculously as finite creatures, wholly unique from the rest of creation and totally dependent upon him. No other creature on earth can compare in terms of personality, communication, creativity, morals, and intelligence—and for good reason—we have been created in the image of our Creator.

Discussion Questions

1. Why is the truth of being created in the image of God important?

2. What do you consider to be the most compelling evidence for our having been created in the image of God?

3. What do you see as problematic with the faith-based theory of the evolution of mankind?

4. Why do you think the account of Adam's naming all the animals was significant?

5. What are some spiritual implications that can be applied to God's creation instruction to all of us to reproduce, reign and reflect?

And all the angels were standing around the throne and around the elders and the four living creatures, and they fell on their faces before the throne and worshiped God, saying, "Amen! Blessing and glory and wisdom and thanksgiving and honor and power and might be to our God forever and ever! Amen."

Revelation 7

At the Top of the World - Beartooth Pass - Montana/Wyoming

Bless the LORD, O you his angels, you mighty ones
who do his word, obeying the voice of his word!

Psalm 103

4

THE UNSEEN WORLD . . .

ministering spirits surrounding us

Our 21st century culture finds itself in a state of continual inner tension. Despite the demand for a godless evolutionary explanation for all things—now deceptively entrenched throughout our society—there still remains a fascination with the possibility of an existing spirit world, and in particular, the presence of angels. The populace's ravenous curiosity regarding the mysterious and unknown continues to drive bookstores to press new and attractive titles describing detailed accounts of personal encounters with otherworldly beings, as well as promising new revelations of what goes on in the unseen world.

This is not one of those books. This book is not going to discuss everything about angels. While the Bible includes many narrative events of angels supernaturally involved in the lives of people, there are particulars that remain unclear at this time. So rather than speculate and try to fill in the blanks, it seems better to readily admit that while God affirms there is an actual angelic host that exists, there are still a lot of unknowns.

With that said, God does expect us to exercise and express our faith in the reality of an unseen spirit world. So what can a person know for sure about angels? The most reliable place to start would be the Word of God, the Bible, carefully examining what it says about angels and their relationship to God as the Creator.

Angels Are Indeed Part of God's Creation

We must bear in mind, angels—although not cut from the same cloth as humans—are wholly dependent upon God just as we are. Angels are not eternal beings. They had a beginning just like us. They rely upon God for their existence. Listen to the apostle Paul's declaration:

> For *by him all things were created, in heaven and on earth, visible and invisible*, whether thrones or dominions or rulers or authorities—all things were created through him and for him. (Colossians 1:16)

Note also that angels are not omniscient—meaning angels do not know all things. They have limitations in their understanding. The apostle Peter reveals this fact in his first epistle:

> *Concerning this salvation*, the prophets who prophesied about the grace that was to be yours searched and inquired carefully, inquiring what person or time the Spirit of Christ in them was indicating when he predicted the sufferings of Christ and the subsequent glories. It was revealed to them that they were serving not themselves but you, in the things that have now been announced to you through those who

preached the good news to you by the Holy Spirit sent from heaven, *things into which angels long to look.* (1 Peter 1:10-12)

The Bible is quite emphatic; there is only one who had no beginning; there is only one who knows all things.

Oh, the depth of the riches and wisdom and knowledge of God! How unsearchable are his judgments and how inscrutable his ways! *"For who has known the mind of the Lord, or who has been his counselor?" "Or who has given a gift to him that he might be repaid?" For from him and through him and to him are all things.* (Romans 11:33-36a)

God's Assignment for Angels

As still more evidence to his commitment to order in creation, we observe in Scripture that God has assigned an angelic rank, if you will, to the angelic host. The Bible often depicts angels having a particular hierarchy dependent upon their celestial role. Here are a few examples:

Michael the Archangel appears to have been given the responsibility of protection over Israel:

At that time shall arise *Michael, the great prince who has charge of your people.* And there shall be a time of trouble, such as never has been since there was a nation till that time. But at that time your people shall be delivered, everyone whose name shall be found written in the book. (Daniel 12:1)

The Angel Gabriel seems to have been given the responsibility of announcement for God:

> "I am Gabriel. I stand in the presence of God, and *I was sent to speak to you* and to bring you this good news." (Luke 1:19b)

Seraphim, uniquely equipped angels as described here, have been given the responsibility of never-ending worship around the throne:

> I saw the Lord sitting upon a throne, high and lifted up; and the train of his robe filled the temple. *Above him stood the seraphim.* Each had six wings: with two he covered his face, and with two he covered his feet, and with two he flew. And *one called to another and said: "Holy, holy, holy is the LORD of hosts; the whole earth is full of his glory!"* (Isaiah 6:1b-3)

Cherubim, bold and powerful angels, were used of God to prevent man from entering back into the Garden of Eden:

> He drove out the man, and at the east of the garden of Eden he *placed the cherubim and a flaming sword* that turned every way to guard the way to the tree of life. (Genesis 3:24)

Cherubim are also described in fairly significant detail in Ezekiel 10 and were also cast as the model for the bowing angels placed atop the Mercy Seat on the Ark of the Covenant (Exodus 25).

Ready, Willing and Able

Angels have purpose for their existence. God's servants (angels) are awe-inspiring spirit beings with great power and ability, completely subject to God's commands. They are not human . . . they are not God. From the text of Scripture we see that angels were created to serve and obey their Creator in at least three different ways:

Ready to Worship

Angels have been God's so-called spiritual cheerleaders (used in reverential fashion) since day one of their creation. They exhibit both a deep reverence and awe in their worship, as well as times of uninhibited shouts of passionate praise and adoration to their Creator. While not all angels look alike, they all have one thing in common: ceaseless worship.

Praise him, *all his angels;* praise him, *all his hosts!* Praise him, sun and moon, praise him, all you shining stars! Praise him, you highest heavens, and you waters above the heavens! Let them praise the name of the LORD! *For he commanded and they were created.* (Psalm 148:2-5)

"Where were you when I laid the foundation of the earth? Tell me, if you have understanding. Who determined its measurements—surely you know! Or who stretched the line upon it? On what were its bases sunk, or who laid its cornerstone, *when the morning stars sang together and all the sons of God shouted for joy?*" (Job 38:4-7)

Day and night they never cease to say, "Holy, holy, holy, is the Lord God Almighty, who was and is and is to come!" (Revelation 4:8b)

A tiny window of what eternity will be like in the presence of our Lord worshiping alongside the angelic host is revealed in the book of Revelation:

Then I looked, and I heard around the throne and the living creatures and the elders the voice of *many angels, numbering myriads of myriads and thousands of thousands, saying with a loud voice,* "Worthy is the Lamb who was slain, to receive power and wealth and wisdom and might and honor and glory and blessing!" (Revelation 5:11-12)

And I saw no temple in the city, for its temple is the Lord God the Almighty and the Lamb. And the city has no need of sun or moon to shine on it, for the glory of God gives it light, and its lamp is the Lamb. By its light will the nations walk, and the kings of the earth will bring their glory into it, and its gates will never be shut by day—and there will be no night there. (Revelation 21:22-25)

It is an awesome thing to consider that one day, everyone who is in Christ will stand in the midst of myriads of angels before the throne of God, and the Lamb in the New Jerusalem, all joining in one voice and one heart eternally thanking our Heavenly Father for his acts of mercy and grace. Until then, the Scriptures tell us that angels are being kept busy, resolved to carry out God's every instruction in preparation for the Final Day.

Willing to Serve

It is evident throughout the Bible that angels are not restricted as to how they look, interact, and perform. They can appear in public or in private, in dreams or in visions, as 'wind and fire' or in the flesh. Their only limitation seems to be what God permits them to do and not do. In God's chain of command, angels serve him on multiple levels, notwithstanding involvement to some degree, with us, his people.

Daniel 10 offers this vivid account of the angel Gabriel sent to assist the prophet Daniel:

Vv. 5-6: I lifted up my eyes and looked, and behold, a man clothed in linen, with a belt of fine gold from Uphaz around his waist. His body was like beryl, his face like the appearance of lightning, his eyes like flaming torches, his arms and legs like the gleam of burnished bronze, and the sound of his words like the sound of a multitude.

Vv. 10-12: And behold, *a hand touched me and set me trembling on my hands and knees.* And he said to me, *"O Daniel, man greatly loved, understand the words that I speak to you, and stand upright, for now I have been sent to you."* And when he had spoken this word to me, I stood up trembling. Then he said to me, *"Fear not, Daniel, for from the first day that you set your heart to understand and humbled yourself before your God, your words have been heard, and I have come because of your words."*

Vv. 18-19: Again one having *the appearance of a man touched me and strengthened me.* And he said, *"O man greatly loved, fear not, peace be with you; be strong and of good courage."* And *as he spoke to me, I was strengthened* and said, "Let my lord speak, for you have strengthened me."

As we see here, often when revealed, an angel's appearance is initially perceived as otherworldly, even terrifying in all its glory. So we should not think it strange for the first words to come out of an angel's mouth to be words of comfort. We see the angelic phrase: "Do not be afraid," or "Fear not," declared again and again throughout Scripture.

The Bible also says that angels may take on the form of a human in order to serve a specific purpose of God. Listen to the writer of Hebrews: "Do not neglect to show hospitality to strangers, for thereby *some have entertained angels unawares"* (13:2). It is apparent there are instances where angels can appear to look like us, male or female (without wings), obediently carrying out God's objective.

There are biblical implications that some angels are assigned to watch over us. Look at what Jesus says in Matthew 18: "See that you do not despise one of these little ones. For I tell you that in heaven *their angels always see the face of my Father* who is in heaven" (v. 10).

Jesus himself had angels attend to him in the wilderness temptation. After fasting for 40 days and withstanding three separate attacks by Satan, Jesus found himself alone in the desert once again, where "*angels came and were ministering to him*" (Matthew 4:11b).

Angels possess intelligence, emotion and curiosity, and all serve with a distinct purpose in mind. It says in Hebrews 1: "Are they not all *ministering spirits sent out to serve for the sake of those who are to inherit salvation?*" (v. 14).

We must not confuse 'sent to serve' with the false notion that we have control over angels, and that we can command them at will to do as we ask. That is an unfounded and unbiblical presumption. The fact is that angels are sent to serve God's intentions in our lives with regard ultimately to our eternal destiny.

Able to Defend

Angels are frequently presented in the Bible as powerful beings almost beyond description. They can be used of God to bring about complete destruction, as well as be placed in a position to serve as a major obstacle, thus preventing attack and destruction from the enemy (Revelation 16:1; 20:1).

To correct a view: Angels don't carry little bows and arrows. No, they usually wield very large swords:

Then the LORD opened the eyes of Balaam, and he saw the angel of the LORD standing in the way, with *his drawn sword in his hand.* And he bowed down and fell on his face. (Numbers 22:31)

And David lifted his eyes and saw the angel of the LORD standing between earth and heaven, and in *his hand a drawn sword* stretched out over Jerusalem. Then David and the elders, clothed in sackcloth, fell upon their faces. (1 Chronicles 21:16)

It is quite evident in God's story that angels are not afraid of direct conflict with evil:

Yet in like manner these people also, relying on their dreams, defile the flesh, reject authority, and blaspheme the glorious ones. But when *the archangel Michael, contending with the devil,* was disputing about the body of Moses, he did not presume to pronounce a blasphemous judgment, but said, "The Lord rebuke you." (Jude 1:8-9)

Then he said to me, "Fear not, Daniel, for from the first day that you set your heart to understand and humbled yourself before your God, your words have been heard, and I have come because of your words. *The prince of the kingdom of Persia withstood me twenty-one days, but Michael, one of the chief princes, came to help me,* for I was left there with the kings of Persia, and came to make you understand what is to happen to your people in the latter days." (Daniel 10:12-14a)

Now war arose in heaven, Michael and his angels fighting against the dragon. And the dragon and his angels fought back, but he was defeated, and there was no longer any place for them in heaven. (Revelation 12:7-8)

79

The Scriptures also remind us that the majority of angels dwell primarily in the spirit-side of creation, serving God. We are not privy to see this unseen reality with the naked eye except on very rare occasion, such as described in this dramatic account found in 2 Kings 6:

> "When the servant of the man of God rose early in the morning and went out, behold, an army with horses and chariots was all around the city. And the servant said, "Alas, my master! What shall we do?" He said, "Do not be afraid, for those who are with us are more than those who are with them." Then Elisha prayed and said, "O LORD, please open his eyes that he may see." So the LORD opened the eyes of the young man, and he saw, and behold, *the mountain was full of horses and chariots of fire* all around Elisha." (2 Kings 6:15-17)

From this historical narrative we learn that there are unique moments of activity when God will permit a person a supernatural glimpse into the spirit world, pulling back the earthly shade and allowing him or her to see things as they really are. It would serve us well to keep in mind that while angels may not be recognized with the human eye, they are always among us, ready, willing, and able to carry out the will of God.

The Great Delusion of the 21st Century

The great pronouncement in this day and age from nearly every worldly media outlet is that the fallen angel—called the Devil in the Bible—is only something we 'religious folk' have conjured up in our minds in order to justify why bad things happen. The media seems intent to dissuade basic Christian beliefs throughout society—promoting instead, a cultural attitude of unbelief. Knowing the truth of Scripture and how the end of time will play out, we should not be too surprised to hear such language from unwitting peddlers of falsehood—that it is silly and childish to believe in such a thing as the Devil. Listen to the apostle John as he penned the book of Revelation: "And the great dragon was thrown down, that ancient serpent, who is called the devil and Satan, *the deceiver of the whole world*" (Revelation 12:9a).

God stands opposed to our culture's confident, yet ignorant assessment that the Devil is a myth. He has told us in his own words that the fallen angel called Satan is quite real and oh so sly. In fact, he is so sly that if we are not careful, we can mistake him for God: "For even *Satan disguises himself as an angel of light.* So it is no surprise if his servants, also, disguise themselves as servants of righteousness" (2 Corinthians 11:14b). This is the darker side of the creation story.

The Scriptures describe a very real diabolical being that labors unceasingly against God's creation in conjunction with his followers (called demons and fallen angels) in order to thwart and destroy anything connected to God. As a part of God's account, we are told of a great rebellion among the angelic host in the heavens. The Devil—a former cherub (ranking angel) as described in Ezekiel 28—and those who chose to rebel with him (all former angels) were cast out of the heavenlies by God, and are now awaiting their eternal punishment.

While our society asserts that the Devil is only a religious fairytale, God's own description of the historical events found in the Bible fits best with what we observe in the current struggle between good and evil.

We are assured from the biblical text that Satan will continue broadcasting a spirit of deception until God decrees:

"Enough!" The Devil's goal, while he has time, is to dupe all of us into the 'big lie' . . . that he is not real, but instead, only a figment of one's imagination. Satan laid it all on the line in his rebellion against God, got it all wrong, and is now paying for it. And he is hell-bent on taking everyone down with him.

For further reading in God's account regarding the origins of evil and the ultimate destination reserved for those who practice evil and unbelief, see the following:

> Genesis 3; Isaiah 14; Ezekiel 28; Revelation 12; Revelation 19-22

Recalibration

Does an unseen world really exist? Is there a real battle between good and evil? Between God and the Devil? Between God's people and the evil horde of demons and fallen angels that follow the Devil? Listen to Paul's assertions:

> For this light momentary affliction is preparing for us an eternal weight of glory beyond all comparison, as we look not to the things that are seen but to the things that are unseen. *For the things that are seen are transient, but the things that are unseen are eternal.* (2 Corinthians 4:17-18)

> For we do not wrestle against flesh and blood, but against the rulers, against the authorities, against the *cosmic powers over this present darkness,* against the *spiritual forces of evil in the heavenly places.* (Ephesians 6:12)

We are in a dangerous winner-take-all battle of life and death, and the angelic host has been sent here to help us. Angels can assume any form as permitted and directed by God. Their focus is to serve and minister to those who choose to follow God. They intervene, protect, help restrain evil, render punishment, and are determined to represent God to man at any time when called upon to do so.

Discussion Questions

1. Why is it imperative to remember that angels are created beings?

2. What do angels look like?

3. What are some cultural misconceptions regarding angels?

4. Why is the existence of the Devil adamantly rejected today?

5. Angels are used of God for what purposes?

God on the Mountain - Superstition Wilderness - Arizona

So you shall know that I am the LORD your God,
who dwells in Zion, my holy mountain.

Joel 3

5

REMOVE YOUR SANDALS . . .

this is holy ground

While God is often described in the Scriptures as mysterious and unconfined; unsearchable and supernatural; the Creator who is eternal, self-existent, and unchangeable; we also discover in the very same pages the incredible truth that God wants us to find him. As travelers on this terrestrial ball, we are encouraged to reach out and seek for our Creator.

And he made from one man every nation of mankind to live on all the face of the earth, having determined allotted periods and the boundaries of their dwelling place, *that they should seek God, in the hope that they might feel their way toward him and find him. Yet he is actually not far from each one of us,* (Acts 17:26-27)

For anyone who would choose to embark upon this journey for God, they will soon discover something quite significant—that God himself has gone the extra mile, providing a supernatural GPS loaded with spiritual waypoints.

Do not miss this; we have been given the inerrant coordinates for locating the one true God, the Creator of all things.

God has declared that not only is he the sovereign Creator, but that he is truly knowable; that the 'knowing' is *not* just for the priest, the pastor, or the prophet. Listen to God in Jeremiah 31: "For they *shall all know me*, from *the least of them to the greatest*, declares the LORD" (v. 34b). God's message today is that each and every person can encounter God on a personal level. God has made himself available in such a way that anyone who would desire a relationship with him can have one. God is not hiding from us.

So, when a person who determines to 'feel their way toward him' actually meets up with the one true God, what might he or she expect as an authentic first encounter? No doubt, an initial exposure to the God of the Bible can produce significant inner conflict. The stark contrast of one's own imperfection in the atmosphere of God's holy perfection is predictable when in such close proximity to the one true God. And while a person may perceive their position in this watershed moment to be disconcerting, humbling, and perhaps even terrifying, the invitation from this holy God remains on the table—to seek him, to find him, and to know him.

The Holiness of God

It is an arduous undertaking for anyone to adequately describe the holiness of God. There is so much depth to the reality of God's holiness that any attempt to move forward should be done so with caution and careful consideration. None of us want to be found spiritually negligent with regard to making God—who is wholly holy—known to others. Still, a biblical understanding of holiness is critical, for holiness defines the nature of God. Holiness is the one facet of God's presence that we all uniformly sense—whether voluntarily or involuntarily—every time we encounter our Creator. Note that a proper assent to God's holy nature is essential, for it is the filter through which we are to apprehend all other characteristics of God, including his love.

Did you know that holiness is the only attribute affixed to God that uses the Hebrew superlative? The word 'superlative' can be defined as *an adjective or adverb describing the highest quality or degree.* In English we use various tools to emphasize a statement, such as an exclamation mark, quotation marks, and terms like, good, better, and best (best being the superlative use of good); again to add emphasis, quality, or degree. In Hebrew—to add emphasis—the writer merely says the word more than once. For instance, we often hear Jesus quoted as saying: "Truly, truly…" This emphatic tool tells the reader or listener they need to pay attention; what is about to be said is very important.

What about the superlative use in Hebrew? Interestingly, to indicate the ultimate emphatic in the Bible, the writer merely says the word or phrase, not two times, but three times! Take a look at the book of Revelation: "Then I looked, and I heard an eagle crying with a loud voice as it flew directly overhead, "*Woe, woe, woe* to those who dwell on the earth, at the blasts of the other trumpets that the three angels are about to blow!"" (8:13). Here you have the superlative used for the word 'woe,' declaring the word three times. We are being told is that this is the ultimate woe—way beyond any other woe.

Using the same tool, we see the word 'holy' in the superlative in Isaiah 6: "*Holy, holy, holy* is the LORD of hosts; the whole earth is full of his glory!" (v. 3b). We see the same emphatic tool also being used for God's holiness in Revelation 4: "*Holy, holy, holy*, is the Lord God Almighty, who was and is and is to come!" (v. 8b).

The use of the superlative to describe God's attribute of holiness provides us with a reliable gauge to appraise its primary importance with regard to our knowing God. Nowhere in the Bible do you find the superlative usage for the love of God, the grace of God, the goodness of God, or the mercy of God. So, when we come across the superlative, *holy, holy, holy*, it should—at the very least—alert us to an aspect of the character of God that necessitates careful consideration and contemplation.

The initial challenge before us when discussing the holiness of God is that the word 'holy' itself is used in so many varied contexts today—some more favorable than others. To clarify for the purpose of understanding here, the word 'holy' in its most basic usage carries with it two nuances: 1) To set apart some person or some thing as wholly unique with intent and purpose. 2) To be morally and spiritually excellent. It is with these definitions that a proper biblical grasp of the word—with regard to God being a holy God—can help expand our own awareness of him. The holiness of God is fully revealed in both definitions. God is transcendent; therefore, he is set apart. God is pure; therefore, he is morally perfect.

The Untouchable Aspect of God's Holiness

We discover in the biblical text that God has revealed himself as uniquely set apart or cut apart from all else—whether terrestrial, ancestral, or celestial. When the word transcendence is attached to the holiness of God, it describes an aspect of God that is incomprehensible, above all, and completely otherworldly. God's transcendence sequesters him from all else to be uniquely God. He has set himself apart from creation as entirely different. He is beyond our own existence. Nothing that has been created can begin to compare with him. Consider these verses that describe the transcendence of God:

There is *no one like* the LORD our God. (Exodus 8:10b)

Therefore you are great, O LORD God. For there is *none like you*, and there is no God besides you, according to all that we have heard with our ears. (2 Samuel 7:22)

There is *none like you*, O LORD; you are great, and your name is great in might. (Jeremiah 10:6)

The transcendence of God also serves as a powerful spiritual waymark to remind us that God is irrefutably sovereign over all things he has created. As he reigns from heaven over all the earth, nothing escapes his notice; nothing happens without his permission; nothing exists apart from his incontrovertible rule emanating from above.

For my thoughts are not your thoughts, neither are your ways my ways, declares the LORD. *For as the heavens are higher than the earth, so are my ways higher than your ways and my thoughts than your thoughts.* (Isaiah 55:8-9)

There is one body and one Spirit—just as you were called to the one hope that belongs to your call—one Lord, one faith, one baptism, *one God and Father of all, who is over all and through all and in all.* (Ephesians 4:4-6)

89

For you, O LORD, are most high over all the earth; you are exalted far above all gods. (Psalm 97:9)

The Unavoidable Aspect of God's Holiness

God is also described in the Bible as morally pure, perfect in all his ways. The writer of Deuteronomy states: "The Rock, *his work is perfect*, for all his ways are justice. A God of faithfulness and *without iniquity*, just and upright is he" (32:4). A presupposition needs to be inserted here: *Exposure to God's holy nature discloses particular moral absolutes in him that are perfect and never change.* It is this moral perfection residing in him that we cannot avoid. The holiness of God confronts the imperfect, the immoral, and the unholy in us. The holiness of God is the realm from which all the laws and commands of God derive their basis for existence. We discover God is a pure God. We discover God is a moral God.

It is not unusual during these divine encounters—when we press in to understand who God is—to find ourselves introspectively confronted with who we really are. Locating our true selves in the midst of our search for God can be a good thing, and at the same time, it can be quite unsettling. Being confronted with the personal aspect of a sovereign transcendent Creator who is morally pure and irreproachable can jar the conscience and rattle the soul. When our lives are measured up against the spiritual plumb line of the holiness of God, reality sets in; we are really not that pure; we are really not that moral.

It is crucial to understand that while in these moments of brushing up against the reality of a holy God, we can, if we are not careful, succumb to a dangerous temptation. Rather than choosing to press forward into knowing God when given the opportunity—which requires authentic transparency on our part—we might be tempted to keep our distance and instead, opt to enter into a conversation of compromise with ourselves; vainly assuring our conscience that a kind God surely must grade his creation on the moral curve. Personally, we know that we haven't measured up, and so we attempt to invalidate the evidence of our shortcomings by confidently asserting that we don't think God will actually judge our actions (or inactions), but that he will instead, reward our life based on the fact that we lived with such great intentions. We only pray this personal assessment of our lives is the case.

But is this really how God works? Listen to these words:

> "*You shall be holy,* for I the LORD your God am holy."
> (Leviticus 19:2b)

> But as he who called you is holy, *you also be holy* in all your conduct, since it is written, "*You shall be holy,* for I am holy"
> (1 Peter 1:15-16)

We see that God's expectation of us as described here is much more than just a pleasant option, nice suggestion, or quaint opportunity. Following God is not just a gobbling up of all his blessings and applying them to all our endeavors. The Bible's clear pronouncement is that God requires that his people be holy, just as he is holy.

A Hard Truth

How prominent is holiness for the Christian? Listen to the writer of Hebrews: "Strive for peace with everyone, and *for the holiness without which no one will see the Lord*" (12:14). The gravity of this statement should be cause for serious self-evaluation;

holiness is the one attribute God declares every single person must both pursue and maintain if anyone would have hope of seeing God. It is clear from this passage that personal holiness is not a choice we get to make, whether to pursue or not to pursue; no, personal holiness is an indispensable requirement of God.

Admittedly, this is not a 'warm fuzzy' moment in Scripture. We are confronted here with the difficult—if not impossible—command to imitate God. And if we don't succeed at it, we are assured we won't ever see God. In other words, if we aren't holy we will never make it to heaven.

This is not unlike other difficult statements found in the Bible. For example, during Jesus' earthly ministry, not long after he had performed the miracle of feeding the five thousand, Jesus tells his listeners that if they do not eat his flesh and drink his blood—the real food of heaven—they will have no life in themselves. Bothered and confused, their reply was understandable: "This is a hard saying; who can listen to it?" (John 6:60b). Had we been there, we, too, might have joined right in with them. But rather than change the message in order to keep the followers happily following, Jesus let the truth stand on its own, and as a result, you have one of the most disappointing events recorded in the Bible, found in John 6:66: "After this many of his disciples turned back and no longer walked with him."

Listen to the words of Jesus once again in Luke 12: "Fear not, little flock, for it is your Father's good pleasure to give you the kingdom. *Sell your possessions, and give to the needy.* Provide yourselves with moneybags that do not grow old, with a treasure in the heavens that does not fail, where no thief approaches and no moth destroys" (Luke 12:32-33). We rationalize the ramifications of such a difficult statement—

Did Jesus really mean what he said? And thus we are quick to conclude—sometimes too quickly—*Surely he doesn't mean for us to willingly become a part of the 'poor populace,' does he?*

The teachings of Jesus can leave an indelible imprint upon us as his truth permeates every single crack and crevice of our lives—baring those most secretive areas that we have so often declared off limits to others—namely our sense of self-justified attitudes and right to privacy. But with God, nothing is off limits. Everything we say, think, do, or have is within his reach. Often we find that our greatest struggle with yielding to God is in these very areas of autonomy, accountability, possessions, and sense of ownership.

Nevertheless, God intends that his truth transform each one of us at the very core of who we think we are. God does not modify truth in order to make it more palatable or workable for us, and as with the difficulty of any statement, there is always the option to reject him and to walk away. But for the one who decides to stick with it and not give up—choosing instead to press forward into knowing him and his ways, God has promised to never leave him or her in the lurch to try to figure things out on their own. His own words of promise can be of real comfort in difficult times like those described above: "I will never leave you nor forsake you" (Hebrews 13:5b).

While hard truths may remain hard truths, such as this passage in Hebrews, it should be noted that this sobering declaration: *"The holiness without which no one will see the Lord,"* although absolutely true, should never be isolated from the rest of Scripture, and from the rest of what God wants us to know about himself. A person left alone with that statement and nothing else of God to hang on to, could find themselves in a spiritual free-fall of hopelessness and despair, because we all know, down deep inside, we just can't measure up to this type of holiness. And yet God requires it. So what is a person to do? Throughout the Bible there are clear implications of the following:

Holiness is a very real possibility: But Jesus looked at them and said, "With man this is impossible, but *with God all things are possible*" (Matthew 19:26).

God has revealed to us our true condition: And no creature is hidden from his sight, but *all are naked and exposed to the eyes of him to whom we must give account* (Hebrews 4.13).

God is not out to nail us in our situation: For *God did not send his Son into the world to condemn the world*, but in order that the world might be saved through him (John 3:17).

In order for us to apprehend a biblical understanding of the necessity of holiness we need see this statement of truth in the context of the message of Christ. Therefore, let's start with the words of Jesus:

"Abide in me, and I in you. As the branch cannot bear fruit by itself, unless it abides in the vine, neither can you, unless you abide in me. I am the vine; you are the branches. Whoever abides in me and I in him, he it is that bears much fruit, for *apart from me you can do nothing*." (John 15:4-5)

It is imperative to believe and live in the knowledge that apart from God, we can accomplish nothing. We must remain connected to him just as branches are to a vine. Branches are wholly dependent upon the vine for nourishment, growth, and fruit. In the same fashion Jesus is telling us that we must 'remain' or 'abide' in him if we are to experience a life-giving relationship with God—which includes the guarantee of eternal life in the realm of God's holiness.

How Do We Become Holy as God is Holy?

It is in this truth of the completed work of Jesus Christ— our vine—that we find our adoptive place in God as sons and daughters of the Most High. The apostle Paul reminds the church of this fact in 1 Corinthians: "And because of him *you are in Christ Jesus, who became to us wisdom* from God, *righteousness* and *sanctification* and *redemption*, so that, as it is written, "Let the one who boasts, boast in the Lord"'" (1 Corinthians 1:30-31). The word 'sanctification' used in this verse can also be translated 'holiness.' Paul is assuring us that what we could never accomplish on our own—to be wise, righteous, holy, and sin-free on our own efforts—Jesus Christ has indeed done for us.

Knowing this truth—regarding the comprehensive work of Christ on our behalf—helps us better understand Jesus' own statement: "*Apart from me you can do nothing*" in John 15:5. The reality is that we have no hope of being holy in the way that God commands us to be holy without the express help of Jesus.

But in order to endow us effectually with the power to be holy, our Lord explained that he would have to first depart this earth so that the Holy Spirit could come to help us. Listen to Jesus' words in the gospel of John: "Nevertheless, I tell you the truth: it is to your advantage that I go away, for if I do not go away, the Helper will not come to you. But if I go, *I will send him to you*" (John 16:7). This Helper Jesus is referring to is also described in the New Testament as the

Spirit of Christ (Romans 8:9) (see the Collaborative Aspect of God in chapter one for a brief discussion of the Trinity; Father, Son, and Holy Spirit).

With Christ as our vine—his energizing Spirit now supplied to us by way of our 'abiding' in him—we can indeed begin to successfully obey God's command—to be holy as he is holy. Being taught and emboldened by the Spirit, we can employ the power we have been given to step out of the mold of this culture, no longer to be coerced by this world's deceptive bias. Instead, we can choose to conduct our lives as God's 'peculiar people' who have been set apart and transformed, eternally dedicated for his purposes. It is in the spirit and power of Christ at work in us that we demonstrate by our holy behavior that we are God's handiwork.

> I appeal to you therefore, brothers, by the mercies of God, to present your bodies as a living sacrifice, holy and acceptable to God, which is your spiritual worship. *Do not be conformed to this world, but be transformed by the renewal of your mind*, that by testing you may discern what is the will of God, what is good and acceptable and perfect. (Romans 12:1-2)

The Word of God tells us that we are to no longer take our cues from the world's directives. This earthly realm is not to be treated as our ultimate destination. Our true home is now with God in Christ. Therefore, mindful of what this aspect of holiness means, we can confidently join in with the saints of Hebrews 11 who understood that they, too, in the power of the Spirit, were different—not cut from the same cloth as the world in which they lived—seeing themselves as true 'strangers and exiles on the earth' (vv. 13-14).

This very same power that compels us to step away from the world's influence also places the moral aspect of holiness within our reach. Through the power of the Spirit we are also afforded the ability to say 'no' to sin. You may recall Jesus telling many of his would-be followers to: "Go and sin no more." In essence he was telling them to stop their sinful behavior—to stop making sinful choices—and instead, be holy as God is holy.

The apostle Paul described this newfound capacity through what some have coined *clothing terminology*. In this new life we now have the authority through Christ to 'take off the old' and 'put on the new' in the same fashion as one would remove and discard soiled garments and replace them with fresh new garments. Paul also likens this process to 'killing off the old man' and 'putting on the new man.' Here are a few passages that can help us understand how we can begin to imitate God in moral purity:

> You have heard about him and were taught in him, as the truth is in Jesus, to *put off your old self,* which belongs to your former manner of life and is corrupt through deceitful desires, and to be renewed in the spirit of your minds, and to *put on the new self,* created after the likeness of God in true righteousness and holiness. (Ephesians 4:21b-24)

> Put to death therefore what is earthly in you: sexual immorality, impurity, passion, evil desire, and covetousness, which is idolatry. On account of these the wrath of God is coming. In these you too once walked, when you were living in them. But now you must put them all away: anger, wrath, malice, slander, and obscene talk from your mouth. Do not lie to one another, seeing that *you have put off the old self* with its practices and have *put on the new self,* which is being renewed in knowledge after the image of its creator. (Colossians 3:5-10)

But I say, walk by the Spirit, and you will not gratify the desires of the flesh. For the desires of the flesh are against the Spirit, and the desires of the Spirit are against the flesh, for these are opposed to each other, to keep you from doing the things you want to do. But if you are led by the Spirit, you are not under the law. Now the works of the flesh are evident: sexual immorality, impurity, sensuality, idolatry, sorcery, enmity, strife, jealousy, fits of anger, rivalries, dissensions, divisions, envy, drunkenness, orgies, and things like these. I warn you, as I warned you before, that those who do such things will not inherit the kingdom of God. *But the fruit of the Spirit is love, joy, peace, patience, kindness, goodness, faithfulness, gentleness, self-control;* against such things there is no law. And those who belong to Christ Jesus have crucified the flesh with its passions and desires. (Galatians 5:16-24)

The possibility of moral purity, just as the ability to step out from under the world's influence, can only be accomplished through the power that Christ provides via his Spirit as we remain in him.

If we live by the Spirit, let us also keep in step with the Spirit. (Galatians 5:25)

Recalibration

There are a number of biblical truths that must come alongside our heavenly Father's command to be holy (1 Peter 1:15):

1. With God all things are possible. (Matthew 19:26)
2. Apart from Jesus we can do nothing. (John 15:4-5)
3. The Helper is here to actually 'help' us. (John 16:7)
4. God is not out to get us. (John 3:17)
5. We have been empowered by the Spirit. (2 Peter 1:3-4)
6. God wants us to share in his holiness. (Hebrews 12:10)
7. God will never leave us nor forsake us. (Hebrews 13:5)

It doesn't matter who we are or what we have done; God yearns for a relationship with us. God, in his boundless compassion, has extended a personal offer: to become our Provision, our Desire, and our Satisfaction. And it is in that moment of God's gracious manifestation that our heart finds its true home in the truth that a holy God desires us. That is true revelation!

Still, it can be quite unnerving to find oneself before his or her Maker, with their soul stripped, unclothed, and exposed, having nothing to offer and nowhere to hide. But what one experiences in that moment of utter vulnerability is startling; he or she discovers that his or her heavenly Father has always been there—waiting patiently for them to return home—no longer to be treated as runaways, but welcomed, clothed with royal garments, forgiven and loved as true sons and daughters—sons and daughters who soon learn that there is really nothing else out there that can compare to what they posses in Christ. Their newfound focus becomes an all-consuming pursuit—they want to be like their Father—they want to be holy because he is holy.

Discussion Questions

1. What makes God a holy God?

2. Why is holiness an often-avoided subject in churches today?

3. How would you describe holiness to another person?

4. Why is holiness a requirement in the life of a follower of God?

5. How can we continue living a holy life in this culture?

The steadfast love of God endures all the day.

Psalm 52

You Are Not Alone - High Desert - Northern Arizona

In that day you will ask in my name, and I do not say to you
that I will ask the Father on your behalf;
for the Father himself loves you

John 16

6

LOVE WITHOUT END . . .

marvelous and extravagant

Jeremiah 31 holds one of the most beautiful truths found in the whole of Scripture. Listen to God's tender message to his people:

> *"I have loved you with an everlasting love;* therefore I have continued my faithfulness to you." (Jeremiah 31:3b)

What splendid words to ponder. What tremendous security this certainty brings us, knowing that God will faithfully continue to act on behalf of those whom he loves because his love never ceases. This is a significant truth we desperately need in this day and age. Its reality can bring great comfort in the midst of the incessant clatter surrounding us—the world shouting a different message—that there is no caring Creator to be found, allegedly supported by the current condition of our planet, which seems now to be spiraling out of control.

An Assessment of the World's Current Status

Since the rebellion of man in the Garden of Eden (recorded in Genesis 3) the world has served as the stage for discord and strife just as God decreed it would. The conflict we experience today is a direct result of humanity's conscious choice to cast off God's rightful rule over every heart and mind.

While mankind's continued disregard for the Creator's call to walk in obedience is really nothing new, it is unmistakable that something unprecedented is happening. We are witnessing an unrivaled intensity of upheaval and discontent throughout the entire globe. The earth and its inhabitants seem to be picking up the pace of discord; displaying a heightened aggravation toward one another as evil tightens its grip upon our world, enticing men and women to think only about themselves and ignore the clear commands of their Creator. God described it like this through the prophet Isaiah some 2,700 years ago: "All we like sheep have gone astray; we have turned—every one—to his own way;" (Isaiah 53:6a).

It is an undeniable reality, there has been a significant increase in failed relationships, lost careers, dried up economies, abandoned homes, homelessness, genocide, tribal wars, terrorist attacks, and devastating catastrophic events. There is evidence on every continent that many people are losing hope. Spirits seem to be drying up, leaving folks with few precious life droplets from which they can only reminisce. And the prospect for the future of this planet doesn't look too promising. The condition of our world, as we know it, is worsening, just as the Bible has predicted would happen.

Regrettably, there are those in the midst of the uncertainty and chaos who confidently assert that the current state of this planet actually proves that there is no God of love, or at the very least, if there is a God, he is either powerless, or he has reneged on his promises. According to the propagandizing efforts of our culture's media—self-appointed prophets who have learned the secret to building an audience through fear-based reporting—this is our present reality.

A Biblical Perspective

Admittedly, the culture's doomsday viewpoint of our world's current condition can seem rather bleak. But from the Bible's vantage point, these life struggles, especially for the Christian, appear to be part and parcel of life here on earth in the midst of the growing tension between good and evil. Listen to God's revelation about what his sons and daughters can expect while here on earth:

"I have said these things to you, that in me you may have peace. In the world you will have tribulation. But take heart; I have overcome the world." (John 16:33)

Beloved, do not be surprised at the fiery trial when it comes upon you to test you, as though something strange were happening to you. (1 Peter 4:12)

Count it all joy, my brothers, when you meet trials of various kinds, for you know that the testing of your faith produces steadfastness. (James 1:2-3)

Blessed is the man who remains steadfast under trial, for when he has stood the test he will receive the crown of life, which God has promised to those who love him. (James 1:12)

The Lord knows how to rescue the godly from trials, and to keep the unrighteous under punishment until the day of judgment, and especially those who indulge in the lust of defiling passion and despise authority. (2 Peter 2:9b-10a)

We are assured that throughout our life of following God there are going to be strategic attempts by the enemy to alienate us from our heavenly Father through difficulty and hardship. We are in a very real battle and while things may seem quite chaotic at the moment, we are informed that we must ready ourselves because the times will become even more difficult as the Final Day nears.

It would be wise to remember that there is an enemy who has always hated God, and because we are God's, that very same enemy hates us. Nothing would delight the Devil more than to see God's own creation turn on him—to hear humanity accuse their Creator that he had failed them. This foe's diabolical obsession is to trick us into believing that our connection with a loving God is all smoke and mirrors, that our alleged relationship is in fact lifeless, and therefore powerless. And while we have the assurance that this is not the case, Satan continues his strategy of deception—defiantly purporting his already lost cause.

To better assist us in understanding what the Bible says will be happening on earth as it makes its way to the Final Day; let's revisit the predictions Jesus made to his disciples. Interestingly, the questions his followers asked of him repeatedly some two thousand years ago are the very same questions we find ourselves asking today: Is the world really going to end? How will it happen? What should we be looking for that will signal the end? How can we prepare for it? Who is going to make it through to the other side? Listen to the words of Jesus in Matthew 24:

> "And *you will hear of wars and rumors of wars*. See that you are not alarmed, for this must take place, but the end is not yet. For *nation will rise against nation, and kingdom against kingdom, and there will be famines and earthquakes in various places*. All these are but the beginning of the birth pains.
>
> Then they will deliver you up to tribulation and put you to death, and you will be hated by all nations for my name's sake. And then *many will fall away and betray one another and hate one another*. And many false prophets will arise and lead many astray. And because lawlessness will be increased, *the love of many will grow cold*. But the one who endures to the end will be saved." (Matthew 24:6-13)

Jesus prophesied that there will be a large number of those who claim to follow God that will fall away, opting instead for a lifestyle consumed with betrayal and hate. Jesus also predicts that the love of many will grow cold—replaced instead by apathy, only thinking of one's self. While Jesus' foretelling of our future in Matthew 24 should affect every hearer, Jesus also instructs those who will listen to take the necessary steps in order to *not* be alarmed.

How does one prevail over the rising uncertainty that now surrounds us? How does one triumph over the fear of the coming calamity? Many would deduce that with everything in the world moving to this prescribed end, how could one be anything but alarmed? So it must be asked: Can a person know genuine peace in the midst of turmoil? Can a person experience a true calm in the midst of catastrophe? Can a person sustain real assurance in the midst of despair?

According to the truth of the Bible, the answer is yes. While we might not see it immediately, there is an important connection between Jesus' prophecy in Matthew 24 and the apostle Paul's description of true love found in 1 Corinthians 13, otherwise known as the 'love chapter.'

The apostle Paul states in 1 Corinthians 13:13: "So now faith, hope, and love abide, these three; but the greatest of these is love." Think about this, why would Paul declare that while faith, hope and love all remain (abide) intact, the greatest of the three, when considered, is to be love? Why is it that love seems to be promoted as superior over faith and hope? Isn't faith and hope just as central in the believer's life? The answer to this question is stated earlier in the chapter. If we aren't careful, we might miss it: "Love bears all things, believes all things, hopes all things, endures all things. *Love never ends*" (1 Corinthians 13:7-8a).

Consider this, while faith, hope, and love are critical components to the Christian life, there is a significant difference between the three with regard to purpose and duration. Bear in mind the fact that there will come a day when faith will no longer be required. Every son and daughter of God has the promise that at the resurrection he or she will see and experience all things as they have been told. From that point forward Christians will physically be in God's presence. There will no longer be a need for a life of faith, for all will receive, in person, what they had believed for—in faith.

The same truth can be applied to the component of hope. At this moment in time we have placed all our hope in him, but there will come a day when hope will be no longer will be needed, for all things hoped for will be actualized. When our day of reward arrives, we will no longer need to continue living our lives in anticipation, longing, and expectation. On that Final Day there will be nothing else for which to hope. Eternal life will be fully established.

While there will come a time when faith and hope will no longer be essential for the Christian life, it is not so with love. This appears to be the reason why the apostle Paul singles out love in 1 Corinthians 13. Love is wholly unique from all else. Love will never ever experience an end to itself like faith and hope, and therefore love can and will endure all things, even the toughest of times.

You recall Jesus declaring in Matthew 24 that the *love of many would grow cold*. Christ was prophesying that it would be the love of men and women, and not the love of God, that will grow cold. The type of love Jesus seems to be describing in this passage is a love that perhaps started out well, but at some difficult point in life, turned stipulatory, focusing upon self-interest and self-preservation rather than upon God.

There are three things a follower of God can count on each waking day: first, times are going to become more and more difficult; second, there will be those around us who will choose to walk away from the faith; third, there is supernatural strength available for those who do not want to give up, so that they may be able to endure to the end.

Let's focus for now on the reality of that third statement, for if we understand Paul's statement, that love will never end and therefore we can have the assurance that love will always endure, we can better grasp the truth and intent of Jesus' statement at the end of his thought: *"But the one who endures to the end will be saved"* (Matthew 24:13). This is where life in God can become much more than mere theory. The type of enduring Jesus is referring to here isn't to be understood as merely trying harder, tolerating more, or braving the hiccups of the world. Endurance for the Christian finds its basis wholly and actively in the love of God.

It is imperative to know that God really does love you and me like no one else can. The type of love God has for every son and daughter is termed *agape* love. The word agape is a Greek word that is translated 'love' in English. It comes from the original language (Koine Greek) that was used to write the New Testament. Agape can be defined as pure selfless love in the highest degree. Unlike other expressions of love found throughout our culture, it is not based on attraction, but upon choice. The agape (love) of God is the most perfect and unconditional display of holy affection one can know. The Bible reminds us that it is with this agape type of love that God has loved us. Therefore, because God has so unreservedly loved us, we too can choose to live a life of love in an agape manner.

The love of God residing in us is personal, purposeful, and powerful, and if we apprehend and express it properly, the love of God will *always* overwhelm the opposition. The enemy will try his best to convince us otherwise, that the love of God can be severed, that it can be terminated, that it can be rendered ineffectual. But the Bible makes it quite clear; the world's cry of chaos and fear mongering is no match for the love of God dwelling in the believer.

For the man or woman who chooses to follow God, he or she is assured that this world will indeed be a difficult place to live, *but it will not be impossible.* In fact, the Bible instructs every Christian to stride this tumultuous planet in victory, as a mighty, yet peaceable, conqueror. We are charged to live life as a true overcomer, understanding that the strength of any victory we experience is found in the omnipotent love of God. For the believer, young or old, abiding in the divine revelation of the love of God can radically alter a person's walk on so many levels. And while there are multi-faceted ways we can explain this type of love, let's examine three particular truths that can significantly bolster our confidence in the supreme love of God at work in us—and its ability to prevail over anything set before us.

The Love of God is an Intimate Love

God reminds us in his word that he is neither prejudice nor partisan. He neither discriminates nor plays favorites. God isn't influenced by whom it is that chooses to try to placate him, no matter the greatness of celebrity status, Christian or non-Christian. The Bible is very clear in its message: 'God is not a man' (Numbers 23:19). Therefore, God does not think or act like we do. The apostle Paul reminded us that God shows no partiality (Romans 2:11).

Joshua—a disciple of Moses and the leader of Israel in their quest for the Promised Land—discovered this impartial characteristic of God firsthand in Joshua 5:

> When Joshua was by Jericho, he lifted up his eyes and looked, and behold, a man was standing before him with his drawn sword in his hand. And Joshua went to him and said to him, *"Are you for us, or for our adversaries?" And he said, "No; but I am the commander of the army of the LORD. Now I have come."* And Joshua fell on his face to the earth and worshiped and said to him, "What does my lord say to his servant?" And the commander of the LORD's army said to Joshua, "Take off your sandals from your feet, for the place where you are standing is holy." And Joshua did so. (Joshua 5:13-15)

The reply is startling. The message is very clear, God will represent himself and his interests alone, regardless of whom it might be that is asking him to take sides. It is this all-powerful and unchallengeable aspect of God that makes the love of the heavenly Father so extraordinary. This impartial, unsearchable God is extending an invitation to the world, to enter into a spiritual journey of unimaginable proportion. God has personally invited us to embark on the mission of a lifetime, to search for and find the One who has loved us with an everlasting love. God seeks a relationship with us, not from a distance, but up close and personal, as a compassionate and attentive Father. Paul put it this way: "That you, being rooted and grounded in love, may have strength to comprehend with all the saints what is *the breadth and length and height and depth, and to know the love of Christ that surpasses knowledge,* that you may be filled with all the fullness of God" (Ephesians 3:17b-19).

Note Paul's aspiration for his readers: "That you may be filled with all the fullness of God." In other words, the ultimate end for every believer is not the *experience* of true love, the *achievement* of personal holiness, a life of *goodness*, countless acts of *kindness*, or a spirit of *gentleness* . . . no, the ultimate goal every follower of God is to be filled with all the fullness of God himself! For that to take place, intimacy must be a possibility.

This is an almost indescribable truth: God desires intimacy with his sons and daughters. That carries with it so many implications. First and foremost, for intimacy to be possible with God we must be rooted and grounded in his love. This is not the same type of love being put on display by the world today. The world's concept of love is temporal, conditional, and often built upon the foundation of sensuality and/or reciprocity. This world has an incessant craving for a sense of self-gratification, which is the primary precondition from which the world will or will not extend its own version of love. What can one get out of loving another? If nothing, then one's love can be, according to the world's way of thinking, justifiably withheld or even withdrawn.

On the other hand, the love of God doesn't begin and end with us, and what we want to get out of it. The love of God rests alone upon God and who he is, both in his character and in his nature. We only love because he first loved us (1 John 4:19). It is a beautiful thing to discover that God's love is neither partial nor conditional, based on who we are or what we do. This type of love portrays a compassionate Creator desiring to give a part of himself to his creation, opening himself up to a relationship with us, simply because he wants to do so. This divine love—when comprehended and put into operation—always results in true intimacy.

What are some reliable indicators that we are moving, or have moved, into intimacy with our Father? Although not a complete list, here are a few expressions of the intimate love that can exist between a son or daughter and their heavenly Father:

- Craving to be in his presence.
- Yearning for conversation.
- Passion to know him.
- Fervor to please him.
- A constant daydreaming about him.
- And of course, as the apostle Paul stated, a hunger to know the breadth, length, heights, and depths (Ephesians 3:18b).

Intimacy with God brings into the light what we—in the dark and separated from God—could have never imagined. God wants to be loved as a Father in the very same way he has loved us as sons and daughters.

The Love of God is an Intentional Love

The love of God is not, as some Christian circles have termed it, 'sloppy agape' or 'greasy grace.' The love of God is not an emotion-fed, free-for-all experience for anyone to do with as they please. The love of God is not to be mishandled, tossed around from person to person, without regard for its intended effect. A *father/son - father/daughter* relationship is what God is after, a familial connection born out of deliberate, fixated love.

The Scriptures assert that God has always had a plan that includes us. Before the foundations of the world were laid, before the blueprints had been drawn up, God purposed to create a people for himself. His motivation? Listen to the apostle Paul:

> Blessed be the God and Father of our Lord Jesus Christ, who has blessed us in Christ with every spiritual blessing in the heavenly places, even as he chose us in him before the foundation of the world, that we should be holy and blameless before him. *In love he predestined us for adoption as sons* through Jesus Christ, *according to the purpose of his will*, to the praise of his glorious grace, with which he has blessed us in the Beloved. (Ephesians 1:3-6)

It is out of love that God has taken the steps required to claim a people for his own. Paul states in Romans 5: "*But God shows his love for us in that while we were still sinners*, Christ died for us" (v. 8).

Our ability to experience the love of God is no longer just a possibility; it is a bold reality, centered on God's unalterable intentions. The redeemed sons and daughters are the indisputable evidence of God's act of redemption, a bold demonstration of the intended purpose of his divine love.

Do not miss this; God's love is focused. It will accomplish its objective: to captivate the hearts of his people and turn them back toward him. May we find assurance in the words of our LORD as declared in Jeremiah 24: "I will give them a heart to know that I am the LORD, and they shall be my people and I will be their God, for *they shall return to me with their whole heart*" (v. 7). Now that's intentional!

The Love of God is an Indestructible Love

Finally, it is helpful to know that God's love dwelling in our hearts is beyond the reach of the enemy. In the midst of our storms, trials, and struggles, we are reassured that the love of God in us will always stand the test of time, because it is permanently grounded in God himself. Paul reminds us of this in Romans:

> Who shall separate us from the love of Christ? Shall tribulation, or distress, or persecution, or famine, or nakedness, or danger, or sword?

> As it is written,
>> "For your sake we are being killed all the day long;
>> we are regarded as sheep to be slaughtered."

> No, in all these things we are more than conquerors through him who loved us. For I am sure that neither death nor life, nor angels nor rulers, nor things present nor things to come, nor powers, nor height nor depth, nor anything else in all creation, will be able to separate us from the love of God in Christ Jesus our Lord. (Romans 8:35-39)

Consider this: Why would the Apostle Paul think it necessary to remind believers of the supremacy of the love of the God in such detailed fashion? Is it because Paul knew that during extreme hardship we would find ourselves tempted to underestimate, or even to forget, the sheer power of the love of God that resides in our hearts?

As Christians, it is good to be reminded regularly from the Word of God of what we actually possess: an unconditional and unlimited lifetime commitment to be loved, which in turn guarantees that the enemy's deliberate attempts to separate God from his sons and daughters will always result in failure. This pledge we have received, this gift of love we hold in our hearts, is irrevocable. The love of God in Christ Jesus is the supernatural 'weld' performed through the giving of the Spirit that keeps our relationship with our God intact, and nothing seen or unseen, physical or spiritual, can break it apart. This truth is founded on the promise God has made to us—that his love never fails!

1 John 3:1a says: "See what kind of love the Father has given to us, that we should be called the children of God; and so we are." We are encouraged to keep in mind that the love of the Father will always protect, defend, and shelter every single son and daughter of his. Listen to the Psalmist's affirmation: "Wondrously show your steadfast love, O Savior of those who seek refuge from their adversaries at your right hand" (Psalm 17:7).

Finally, we must not overlook the supreme proof that this agape form of love is genuine, and freely available for every son and daughter. It is most appropriately described in what is perhaps the most familiar verse found throughout the Bible:

For God so loved the world, that he gave his only Son, that whoever believes in him should not perish but have eternal life. (John 3:16)

Jesus Christ's life, death, and resurrection irrefutably authenticated the everlasting love of our heavenly Father. Through this compassionate act of love, God has shown himself to be, not only eternal in nature, but also indestructible; the one who has triumphed on our behalf over all our enemies, even our greatest of foes—death itself.

"Death is swallowed up in victory.
O death, where is your victory?
O death, where is your sting?" (1 Corinthians 15:54b-55)

Recalibration

To be sure, there will continue to be conflict and struggle in this world. We live in the midst of a selfish, self-centered, look-out-for-number-one people. God tells us to avoid being overcome by that type of spirit, but instead, let the intimate, intentional, and indestructible love of God rule in our hearts—demonstrating before a watching world that true victory over all things can be experienced through the love of God in Christ. God desires us to first know and experience his love for ourselves, and then, having been personally convinced of its life-giving power, testify to others, inviting them to surrender their lives to the sovereign supremacy of his love.

The decision to make this journey has attached to it a number of life-altering implications: Am I prepared to let God, in love, show me who I really am? Am I willing to be changed, transformed from within, by the life-giving power

117

of his love? Am I ready to receive new eyes, to see the world—and beyond—as I never have before?

We do have a decision to make. Yes, we can choose to try to make it through this existence on our own, but the consequence of this life-choice is to find ourselves repeatedly cast back onto the same lifeless landscape full of lost opportunities. One must confess that is a pretty hopeless place to find oneself, choosing the lure of an empty life devoid of authentic love with not much of a future beyond a few decades. Thankfully, because of the love of God, we do have another option.

God has reached out to us in the role of a Father who ardently loves his sons and daughters. The Father offers every child of God true intimacy—something we all crave. He assures his children that this love relationship is very intentional; that it is a something he has wanted from the beginning. And he declares that no one or no thing can touch or destroy this love relationship, because it is God's own omnipotent love that holds it in its place, secured for all eternity. Now that's a love worth pursuing, worth having, and worth sharing.

Discussion Questions

1. What is the world's version of true love?

2. Why does the enemy want to invalidate the love of God?

3. Why is intimacy with God essential?

4. Why does the love of God need to be described as powerful?

5. How does one know if they have the love of God in their lives?

Annular Solar Eclipse - May 20, 2012 – Fish Creek Hill - Arizona

Therefore the LORD waits to be gracious to you, and
therefore he exalts himself to show mercy to you.
For the LORD is a God of justice;

Isaiah 30

7

MERCY AND JUSTICE . . .

the whole counsel of God

What you personally believe about God matters. What your family and friends believe about God matters. What your colleagues and acquaintances believe about God matters. What every single person you encounter believes about God matters. It matters because God has told us that there are eternal consequences attached to what a man or woman chooses to believe about him.

For the Christian, the concept of belief is much more than just a matter of offering mental assent to someone or something. A simple cognitive nod, conceding God's existence is woefully inadequate when it comes to the Creator of the universe. Unfortunately, our culture doesn't buy into that truth. In today's society, *what* a person believes really isn't an issue. In fact, we are assured that it is not necessary to believe in anything at all. In most secular circles, unbelief is just as valid as belief. This is not so for the follower of God.

Let's take this a step further. It is fundamental that what we believe about God be correct. Jesus declared that on the

Last Day there would be many standing before him who will have every expectation of being ushered right into heaven, but to their astonishment it will be revealed that their erroneous assumptions would be in fact the very grounds for their disqualification:

> *"Not everyone who says to me, 'Lord, Lord,' will enter the kingdom of heaven,* but the one who does the will of my Father who is in heaven. On that day many will say to me, 'Lord, Lord, did we not prophesy in your name, and cast out demons in your name, and do many mighty works in your name?' And *then will I declare to them, 'I never knew you; depart from me, you workers of lawlessness.'"* (Matthew 7:21-23)

The alarming declaration of Jesus—that there will be those who will assume, *even up to the very last minute*, that what they believed about God was good enough, only to discover that their manner of belief and practice was deficient—is intended to serve as an early warning sign for those of us listening so we can personally evaluate our own lives and thus avoid the same demise. This is why every single follower of God must be oh so careful that they do not find themselves believing in—or presenting to others—a notion of a *'half-a-god'* system of belief, which is really not God at all. Let's clarify what is meant by the phrase, half-a-god.

In Acts 20, the apostle Paul, having called for a personal meeting with the elders of the church of Ephesus, sensed the express need to sum up his ministry among them, knowing that he would not see them again. Listen to Paul's own words:

> "You yourselves know how I lived among you the whole time from the first day that I set foot in Asia, serving the

Lord with all humility and with tears and with trials that happened to me through the plots of the Jews; *how I did not shrink from declaring to you anything that was profitable*, and teaching you in public and from house to house, testifying both to Jews and to Greeks of repentance toward God and of faith in our Lord Jesus Christ." (Acts 20:18b-21)

Paul continues on in vss. 25-28:

"And now, behold, I know that none of you among whom I have gone about proclaiming the kingdom will see my face again. Therefore I testify to you this day that I am innocent of the blood of all, for *I did not shrink from declaring to you the whole counsel of God*. Pay careful attention to yourselves and to all the flock, in which the Holy Spirit has made you overseers, to care for the church of God, which he obtained with his own blood." (Acts 20:25-28)

Note several important assertions in these verses:

1. Paul did not have permission to shorten up or modify the message of God.
2. He truly believed that every single truth about God was beneficial for his listeners.
3. For the mission to be considered complete, it had to include the whole counsel of God.
4. Paul's commitment to make known all of God's counsel while he still had breath provided the opportunity for a personal declaration of innocence (a clear conscience); that Paul himself had believed properly and had faithfully communicated God to his hearers, thus disqualification was not an issue.

Think for a moment . . . What is Paul referring to when he mentions the whole counsel of God? From the passage itself we can learn the following: Ignoring portions of the Bible while choosing to focus upon preferred truths to which we are personally attracted will not produce an authentic view of God, nor can it result in a proper representation of him. Choosing to disregard select aspects of who God is can be tantamount to hiding a part of him from those with whom we would speak. The message in its entirety—both the wonderful aspect of God as our attentive heavenly Father, as well as uneasy aspects of God as our Maker who will hold us accountable for all we think, say, and do—is to be understood as the whole counsel of God and therefore should be considered as profitable for all.

Declaring the whole counsel of God is not a responsibility reserved solely for the expert Bible teacher. God expects every single son and daughter of his to first, believe, and then to present who he is as laid out in all of Scripture.

There is much more to our personal responsibility— presenting the whole counsel of God—than just an assignment of living a particularly Jesus-like lifestyle before others, assuming that those who observe us will naturally want to get to God through some sort of spiritual osmosis emanating from our being. Some have actually come to believe that a person's life can be so profoundly lived before others that a single word should not have to be uttered. If that were the case, Jesus, the most profound person to have ever occupied this planet, should never have had to say a single thing. Yet, there he was, God incarnate, explaining, correcting, confronting, rebuking, defending, praying, comforting, affirming, and loving, using the spoken word—

the whole counsel of God—to reveal, convince, and convict, then backing up every single word with action.

One might be tempted to respond, "Well that was Jesus and I'm not him." Remember, the apostle Peter told us that Jesus has left us an example and that we should follow in his steps (1 Peter 2:21). Paul also reminds us that we should resolve to be imitators (1 Corinthians 11:1). Therefore, if we are going to imitate Jesus, then content does matter. And the content cannot be just any random concept of God we might conjure up; it must be content from the Word of God, the very words Jesus lived by.

Thus we arrive at a basic, yet often-uncomfortable subject: the mercy and justice of God. We cannot escape the fact that the whole counsel of God must include facets that exist on both ends of the spiritual spectrum: his being the gentle Savior and retributive Judge, the forgiving Father and immutable Creator, the compassionate Counselor and the absolute Ruler. This is the very area where some run the risk of trying to construct and present a half-a-god system of belief. There are those who are not comfortable with the reality of the justice of God, therefore they assume that if they can merely overwhelm the message of the Christian faith with mercy, love, longsuffering, and goodness, then the need of making known the justice of God will in fact become a non-issue. This is one of those 'shrinking back' instances Paul spoke of in Acts 20, withholding certain aspects of God that are actually to be seen scripturally as profitable for all.

In light of our content needing to be correct content in order for it to be valid content, and in light of our personal responsibility to make all of God known, it would do us well to attempt to understand what Paul means when he says: "I did not shrink from declaring to you the whole counsel of

God," rather than making a concerted effort to distance ourselves from this particular teaching.

To better apprehend what Paul is saying, let's consider another of Paul's comments with regard to the whole counsel of God:

> *Note then the kindness and the severity of God*: severity toward those who have fallen, but God's kindness to you, provided you continue in his kindness. (Romans 11:22)

Paul instructs us to take into account, ponder and give special attention to both God's kindness and God's severity. If we hold to the divine inspiration of Scripture, then we can conclude that God himself is telling us to carefully note both his kindness and his severity. Many would prefer to ignore the truth of God's severity and just immerse everyone with kindness. But we are not privy to picking and choosing what we like and don't like in the Bible, and thus presenting accordingly, especially when you have a statement like this one that starts with: "Note then ..." So, biblically speaking, we do not have the option to ignore the truth of the severity, i.e., the justice of God. We have been given the responsibility to fully declare all God has revealed, earnestly warning others, yet without personal attack or vengeful anger.

Let's bring in yet another passage from Paul's writings to further assist us in understanding the concept of the whole counsel of God:

> Or do you presume on the riches of his kindness and forbearance and patience, not knowing that *God's kindness is meant to lead you to repentance*? But because of your hard and impenitent heart you are storing up wrath for yourself on

the day of wrath when God's righteous judgment will be revealed. (Romans 2:4-5)

When Paul states that we are to note the kindness and severity of God in Romans 11, it is probable that he has this concept in mind; *the kindness of God is intended to lead a person to repentance.* We must remember that it is kindness that draws a person to God, not severity. The severity of God is the consequence of an impenitent heart, of one who has chosen to reject the kindness of God, preferring not to repent, believe, and be reconciled back to God. In other words, for the person who persists in unbelief, ignoring God's remedy for restoration, there will *always* be consequences.

The Need for Uncensored and Uncut Content

The underlying principles presented throughout this book have been thus: God expects to be accurately understood and intimately experienced by the sons and daughters of Adam and Eve. We've discussed at some length the foundational aspects of God that are central to knowing the truth about him: He is the sovereign Creator of all things; he is completely holy and desires his followers to share in that holiness; and that he has unconditionally loved those whom he has called his own with an omnipotent and everlasting love. Those are fundamental factors to take into account when considering whom the one true God is.

In the same fashion, being aware of both God's mercy and justice will greatly help bring the revelation of God into better focus. Our heavenly Father wants us to know that there is a danger of focusing on one aspect of himself at the expense of the other. God is not so vehemently severe—out to get his pound of rebellious flesh—that no man or woman in his creation stands a chance. At the same time, God is not so obligingly permissive—inattentive to our naughtiness—that he chooses to merely wink at our persistent disobedience. Therefore, it is imperative that we examine both the mercy and justice of God. By investigating the biblical truth of mercy and justice, it is the hope that any previous misgivings regarding God's sovereign rule over creation will be brought into a proper balance.

Justice . . . a Right of God

In an attempt to improve our perception of God's justice as described in the Bible, it would be of great benefit to first expunge a few biased views; namely, the assumption that our own governmental systems are a direct reflection of how God works (or vice versa). While there are many truths taken from Judeo-Christian teachings that have influenced the formation of governments throughout the world, we don't want to fall prey to forcing a particular system back upon how God works.

To begin, there are not distinct governing branches in God's economy. God is himself the Lawmaker, Ruler, and Judge over the whole earth. There are no elected officials with term limits in God's economy. He neither rules by popular opinion nor by majority vote. Lobbyists don't have access to him. Politics do not affect his decisions. There is not the option that, if citizens don't like the law, they can enter a legislative process in order to get the law changed. There is no appellate court in God's domain. There is never a campaign year with God, whereby he might promise something, of which he may or may not deliver. God makes good on his promises 100% of the time!

It is when we start assuming that God and his ways are analogous to our existing government that we run into direct conflict with the truth of the sovereignty of God and his exercise of justice. This tension can be intensely felt when there is a clash between an individual's requisite for personal freedom and the truth of accountability to someone higher than themselves. For example, when a person asks for prayer, they might hastily agree that God is in control and therefore petition God to work on their behalf. But then just as quickly, they might turn cold and rigid when confronted with the truth of God's sovereign rule over them outside of this specific prayer request.

When a person maintains that there be wiggle room with God, that there be inalienable times of autonomy when the divine Eyes are not watching them, they are merely demonstrating their underlying desire to have the right to be god-like, to make their own sovereign choices. The assumption that every person is entitled to self-governing control over his or her own life was the initial problem in the Garden. Did you know that the choice to rely upon our own self-made system of right and wrong, preferring our life view over God's own perfect counsel is the very reason people die every single day? That's right! As a part of his creation, we are living out—the act of dying—the very decree of the One who made us.

> The LORD God took the man and put him in the garden of Eden to work it and keep it. And the LORD God commanded the man, saying, "You may surely eat of every tree of the garden, but of the tree of the knowledge of good and evil you shall not eat, for in the day that you eat of it you shall surely die." (Genesis 2:15-17)

Therefore, just as sin came into the world through one man, and death through sin, and so death spread to all men because all sinned— (Romans 5:12)

The Creator has informed his creation, through the truth of the Bible, this is how things work. Some would like to conclude that since they were not personally in the garden, they therefore should not be held personally responsible for Adam's act of disobedience. We must not forget that Adam was God's sovereign choice as the one who would represent all mankind. If Adam had not disobeyed, we can surmise that death would not have entered the world, but such was not the case. What has happened has happened. It is a bell that cannot be 'unrung.' Death is now a reality for us all.

Still, some will cry out, "That's just not fair!" We must come to grips with the fact that *fairness* is not a doctrine of God. It is a manmade idea that individuals should be treated a certain way; according to one's own felt sense of right and wrong in the moment. It is purely relative, based on how we personally think things should be. Fairness does not draw from the absolutes of God's decree of what is truly right and what is truly wrong.

For some, discovering the truth that their idea of fairness actually stands juxtaposed to the reality of God's justice is a considerable dose of bad news. Believe it or not, that is a good place to be, for without our being confronted with the truth of the bad news and our own desperate situation before our Creator, any good news we might receive won't really serve as good news. Instead, it will only exist as something to be gobbled up from God's benevolent hand in order to serve our own interests. The good news of God must always be heard and understood through the filter of the bad news of man. The Bible's disclosure of the bad news will also go a long way to answering the questions we often ponder about why we do what we do and why evil exists.

The Bad News

1. God has declared that every single person is a sinner. It is imperative to recognize that the Creator has not left a soul out of this unpleasant appraisal of humanity:

> As it is written:
> None is righteous, no, not one; no one understands; no one seeks for God. All have turned aside; together they have become worthless; no one does good, not even one. Their throat is an open grave; they use their tongues to deceive. The venom of asps is under their lips. Their mouth is full of curses and bitterness. Their feet are swift to shed blood; in their paths are ruin and misery, and the way of peace they have not known. There is no fear of God before their eyes. (Romans 3:10-18)

And to remove all doubt about who is included in this assessment, the apostle Paul drives home the point a few verses later in the chapter:

> For there is no distinction: for all have sinned and fall short of the glory of God, (Romans 3:22b-23)

Not a very flattering description of mankind, for sure. And while it would betray God to try and bypass such a foundational truth about man, it is understandable why some elect to try and do so. The reality of man's sin before his God is not a popular subject. People aren't instinctively attracted to it. By nature, we do not like to be called out from our place of privacy (which the Bible defines as darkness) into the light, fully disclosing who we truly are, where pretense, façade, and self-reliance have no footing.

Still, there are those who will insist that they not be included in such an odious lot. Sin, so they believe, is reserved for the really bad people, not for those who work hard and raise a good family, or so the tale goes, which leads us right into our second piece of bad news.

2. We are not permitted to come up with our own definition of sin. God has clearly described for us what sin is. Interestingly, his definition of the types of sin that actually exist may be of surprise to some.

First, sin is defined as choosing to live our life in willful disobedience—through acts of defiance—as if there is no law of God to obey. The apostle John declares:

> Everyone who makes a practice of sinning also practices lawlessness; sin is lawlessness. (1 John 3:4)

This type of sin is obvious to most. Active disobedience to the law of God is sin. Murders, adultery, robbery, are discernably sinful acts. But we cannot overlook the fact that there is a passive side to this lawlessness as well. Living our life according to our own self-generated moral compass, while ignoring God and his ways, is also considered sin.

> For whatever does not proceed from faith is sin. (Romans 14:23b)

A life lived apart from faith in God is sin. The entire eleventh chapter of Romans asserts that God's severity is reserved for those who refuse to believe and have faith in him. It is crucial that we recognize that sin isn't defined solely as outwardly aggressive acts of disobedience. Just the simple act of unbelief—the absence of faith—is considered sin in God's eyes.

One other sin is identified in the Bible, termed by many as the 'sin of omission.' The definition is found in the book of James:

> So whoever knows the right thing to do and fails to do it, for him it is sin. (James 4:17)

So we see that sin is not merely assigned to the things we do, sin is also defined by the things we don't do. Knowing what is right and refusing to respond in obedience is in itself an act of disobedience. In other words, doing nothing is also sin. God has made it quite clear; he requires action, not passivity, on our part.

3. All have been born with a sin nature. We entered this life at birth wholly consumed with ourselves. From day one our cravings have been all about us. Our parents did not have to teach us to say, "*Mine!*" That came naturally. Our parents did not have to teach us to say, "*I want that!*" That came naturally. Our parents did not have to teach us to say, "*Me! Me! Me!*" That came naturally. Our parents did not have to teach us to disobey. That came naturally.

David described mankind's birth condition in Psalm 51:

> Behold, I was brought forth in iniquity, and in sin did my mother conceive me. (Psalm 51:5)

The moment we took our first breath, we revealed our determination to be number one. We were birthed in a state of rebellion against anything that wasn't about us. This abnormal condition—compared to the normal condition of creation before sin entered the world—is described in practical fashion in 1 John:

> For all that is in the world—the desires of the flesh and the desires of the eyes and pride of life—is not from the Father but is from the world. (1 John 2:16)

Our consolation, if there were any, would be that every single person coming into this world—biblically speaking—is born in that very same condition.

4. We are going to die because of sin. For many men and women there is a fearful grip of finality in death. It is the unfamiliar place where there are no second chances. Death is the moment where a person's eternal reward—good or bad— is actualized. We wish we could avoid death, but as part of God's disobedient creation, it is inevitable. This is the consequence for our sin.

> For the wages of sin is death, (Romans 6:23a)

And again, the writer of Hebrews declares:

> And just as it is appointed for man to die once, and after that comes judgment, (Hebrews 9:27)

For anyone who would refuse to believe this truth about sin and death, God has graciously laid out the requirements they would need to fulfill in order to avoid the penalty of death and thereby experience eternal life. A person would have to be in perfect obedience to God every single moment of every single day of their existence, without a single slip-up. As we are all aware, this is an impossible feat. We are all guilty. James states it this way:

> For whoever keeps the whole law but fails in one point has become accountable for all of it. (James 2:10)

Let's put to rest the notion that eternal life is possible through one's own success in obedience. The evidence of our disobedience remains on all of us—for we all die.

5. *Fairness has nothing to do with it.* When one pulls the 'Not Fair!' card, they are declaring that in some form or fashion that God is not doing things as they think he should. They are, in essence, questioning God's right to exercise his justice. Paul deals with this very issue in Romans 9:

> *What shall we say then? Is there injustice on God's part? By no means!* For he says to Moses, "I will have mercy on whom I have mercy, and I will have compassion on whom I have compassion." *So then it depends not on human will or exertion, but on God, who has mercy.* For the Scripture says to Pharaoh, "For this very purpose I have raised you up, that I might show my power in you, and that my name might be proclaimed in all the earth." *So then he has mercy on whomever he wills, and he hardens whomever he wills.*
>
> You will say to me then, "Why does he still find fault? For who can resist his will?" *But who are you, O man, to answer back to God?* Will what is molded say to its molder, "Why have you made me like this?" Has the potter no right over the

clay, to make out of the same lump one vessel for honorable use and another for dishonorable use? What if God, desiring to show his wrath and to make known his power, has endured with much patience vessels of wrath prepared for destruction, in order to make known the riches of his glory for vessels of mercy, which he has prepared beforehand for glory— (Romans 9:14-23)

Bottom line, God may do exactly as he pleases and we may not cry, "Foul!" God is perfectly just in all things. He, being the Creator, is privileged to set the rules and regulations for eternal life and the consequences for disobedience. Gratefully, there are neither unjust judgments nor erroneous decisions on the part of God. He's not in the business of rendering 'fair or unfair' verdicts. We have the assurance that every single one of us will receive a just and righteous ruling at the end of our lives for everything we've said, done, and thought—for every action—and inaction.

Let's review two other biblical accounts regarding the justice of God over and against the fairness concept. One is a conversation Jesus had with Peter after the resurrection:

"Truly, truly, I say to you, when you were young, you used to dress yourself and walk wherever you wanted, but when you are old, you will stretch out your hands, and another will dress you and carry you where you do not want to go." (This he said to show by what kind of death he was to glorify God.) And after saying this he said to him, "Follow me."
Peter turned and saw the disciple whom Jesus loved following them, the one who also had leaned back against him during the supper and had said, "Lord, who is it that is going to betray you?" When Peter saw him, he said to Jesus, "Lord, what about this man?" Jesus said to him, *"If it is my*

will that he remain until I come, what is that to you? You follow
me!" (John 21:18-22)

Peter's comment is quite plausible. He's just been told he's
going to die for the cause of Christ. Peter then looks over to
the apostle John and says, "What about him?" [my
paraphrase]. Peter seemed to be looking at this situation from
the reference point of fairness. Jesus corrected his perception
by declaring that what would happen with John was really
none of his business. Peter was told, instead, to focus all his
energies on following him.

Again, we see this same idea in a parable Jesus told:

"For the kingdom of heaven is like a master of a house who
went out early in the morning to hire laborers for his
vineyard. After agreeing with the laborers for a denarius a
day, he sent them into his vineyard. And going out about the
third hour he saw others standing idle in the marketplace,
and to them he said, 'You go into the vineyard too, and
whatever is right I will give you.' So they went. Going out
again about the sixth hour and the ninth hour, he did the
same. And about the eleventh hour he went out and found
others standing. And he said to them, 'Why do you stand
here idle all day?' They said to him, 'Because no one has
hired us.' He said to them, 'You go into the vineyard too.'
And when evening came, the owner of the vineyard said to
his foreman, 'Call the laborers and pay them their wages,
beginning with the last, up to the first.' And when those
hired about the eleventh hour came, each of them received a
denarius. Now when those hired first came, they thought
they would receive more, but each of them also received a
denarius. And on receiving it they grumbled at the master of
the house, saying, 'These last worked only one hour, and you
have made them equal to us who have borne the burden of

the day and the scorching heat.' But he replied to one of them, 'Friend, I am doing you no wrong. Did you not agree with me for a denarius? Take what belongs to you and go. I choose to give to this last worker as I give to you. Am I not allowed to do what I choose with what belongs to me?'" (Matthew 20:1-15a)

The assertion once again is that God does not work from the concept of fairness. He is not bound to an across the board union or minimum wage law. He does not have to pay overtime. He does not evaluate human beings on some sort of man-oriented moral curve. God will do what God wants to do because he is above all. He is not like us, nor does he pretend to be. God is just because he has the right to be just and thus has the right to hold his creation accountable. He made all things, he sustains all things, and he will be the one who will determine the ultimate outcome of all things.

Who Can Stand?

Here is a summary of the bad news. God has defined the rules of life by which we must obey or die. Our best efforts to fulfill his requirements will never be good enough to earn the reward of eternal life. We will indeed be held accountable for every slip-up. Jesus said: "I tell you, on the day of judgment *people will give account for every careless word they speak*, for by your words you will be justified, and by your words you will be condemned" (Matthew 12:36-37). All of us have been born with a sin nature and therefore we are all considered sinners before God. We didn't have a choice about our condition. God will not permit us to counter with, "That's just not fair!" Paul's statement in Romans 9 is echoed once again: "But who are you, O man, to answer back to God?" (Romans 9:20a).

And so . . . we have no legitimate reply. We only find ourselves confronted with the undeniable justice of the one true God:

> Now we know that whatever the law says it speaks to those who are under the law, so that every mouth may be stopped, and *the whole world may be held accountable to God.* (Romans 3:19)

> But the LORD sits enthroned forever; he has established his throne for justice, *and he judges the world with righteousness; he judges the peoples with uprightness.* (Psalm 9:7-8)

> For the LORD loves justice; he will not forsake his saints. They are preserved forever, but the children of the wicked shall be cut off. (Psalm 37:28)

Now, if the story ended here, there would only be cause for despair and despondency. If this were the sum of our existence, then we should join in with the rest of the world declaring: "Let us eat and drink, for tomorrow we die." But thanks be to the living God, the story doesn't end here. Against the backdrop of this report of bad news—which is, in truth, God merely exercising his right to be just—there is some really, really good news to be shared!

> I waited patiently for the LORD; he inclined to me and heard my cry. He drew me up from the pit of destruction, out of the miry bog, and set my feet upon a rock, making my steps secure. He put a new song in my mouth, a song of praise to our God. Many will see and fear, and put their trust in the LORD. (Psalm 40:1-3)

Mercy . . . a Choice by God

Declaring the truth of the justice and severity of God and thus exposing the human race's guilt before their Creator is not to be treated with disdain; as if this aspect of God's truth is something we must continually hide from people or be embarrassed about. Paul reminds us that it is essential to faithfully share the *whole counsel of God,* and not just select portions of truth, for all of it is beneficial.

Now, with regard to the justice of God, consider this: Why doesn't this righteous and just God go ahead and wipe us out and be done with all the sin and rebellion? Not that we would want him to do so (obviously if this were the case I would not be sitting here penning this book, and you would not be sitting where you are reading it), but if truth were told, God has every right to call it quits with his creation . . . yet he hasn't. Why is that?

It is because while God exercises justice by right, God is merciful by choice. Yes, it is the sheer kindness of God that keeps us from coming under the immediate execution of his judgment. Clearly, in light of the bad news revealed earlier in this chapter, we don't deserve his kindness. Our persistent narcissism hasn't earned his favor. It is only because of God's tender mercy for us that we are here today, a gracious act that we are to never take for granted. You recall this passage from earlier in the chapter:

> Or do you presume on the riches of his kindness and forbearance and patience, not knowing that *God's kindness is meant to lead you to repentance*? But because of your hard and impenitent heart you are storing up wrath for yourself on the day of wrath when God's righteous judgment will be revealed. (Romans 2:4-5)

To remove any misconception, the kindness of God does not exist so we may insolently revel in our disobedience all the while assuming he'll tolerate our misbehavior in a permissive fashion because he's such a kind God. No, the kindness of God has taken aim at us with a single goal in mind. The kindness of our Maker has been extended to human race for the express purpose of leading men and women into repentance toward God. That's it! The goal of his kindness is to get us back into right relationship with him. The kindness of God will not lead you anywhere else. If you land in some other spot than a truly repentant heart, then it's not the kindness of God at work in your life. It is another spirit busily at work to get your focus off of your true condition before your Maker.

Repentance is the first step every person—young or old, rich or poor—must make toward God. To ignore repentance or try to come up with another alternative—such as working hard and living right—in order to gain God's favor would be to presume upon his established truth. Repentance is not something we can simply ignore. Repentance is not only reserved for certain people (those whom we think really need it). It is the message every man and woman in creation must first hear and then act upon. Let it be said, it is not enough to just hear the message of repentance. Action is required. This is not something new. Repentance was the leading subject both Jesus and his disciples addressed with their listeners throughout their ministries as described in the New Testament:

"Repent, for the kingdom of heaven is at hand." (Matthew 3:2; 4:17b)

So they went out and proclaimed that people should repent. (Mark 6:12)

"I have not come to call the righteous but sinners to repentance." (Luke 5:32)

"No, I tell you; but unless you repent, you will all likewise perish." (Luke 13:3, 5)

"Repentance and forgiveness of sins should be proclaimed in his name to all nations, beginning from Jerusalem." (Luke 24:47b)

And Peter said to them, "Repent and be baptized every one of you in the name of Jesus Christ for the forgiveness of your sins," (Acts 2:38)

"Repent therefore, and turn back, that your sins may be blotted out," (Acts 3:19)

"The times of ignorance God overlooked, but now he commands all people everywhere to repent," (Acts 17:30)

"But declared first to those in Damascus, then in Jerusalem and throughout all the region of Judea, and also to the Gentiles, that they should repent and turn to God," (Acts 26:20a)

As we can see from just these few verses (there are many more), repentance is the initial message God is speaking to us. It is unavoidable. Our being given the opportunity to repent toward God and make things right with him is in point of fact the kindest thing our Maker could have done for us. True repentance provides a way back to a right relationship with

God and is our entry point into the hope of eternal life. It is the only path to true forgiveness for our sin. Repentance is what converts bad news into good news.

If you are serious about your relationship with God, which I assume you are since you are reading this book, you may have some questions about now for which you'd like some answers:

- From God's vantage point, what does true repentance look like?
- What is actually involved in truly repenting?
- How will I know if I've done it right and not just gone through the motions?

Psalm 32 provides one of the clearest pictures found in all of Scripture of what authentic repentance looks like. The Psalm reads:

¹Blessed is the one whose transgression is forgiven,
    whose sin is covered.
²Blessed is the man against whom the LORD counts no iniquity,
    and in whose spirit there is no deceit.
³For when I kept silent, my bones wasted away
    through my groaning all day long.
⁴For day and night your hand was heavy upon me;
    my strength was dried up as by the heat of summer. Selah
⁵I acknowledged my sin to you,
    and I did not cover my iniquity;
I said, "I will confess my transgressions to the LORD,"
    and you forgave the iniquity of my sin. (Psalm 32:1-5)

It is fundamental to recognize that genuine conviction precedes true repentance. Reread verses three and four. King David, the writer of this song, describes in detail what it was like in his own personal struggle while under the conviction of the Spirit of God. His attempts to keep silent or ignore the Spirit's conviction affected every single aspect of his life, both in his physical body and in his spirit. No matter where he went he could not locate a 'peaceful retreat' to quiet his conscience. It dogged him all day long. It hounded him in his sleep. When he awoke the groaning was still pounding in his ears. He could not make it go away. He was quickly learning that he could not escape God. David experienced the full weight of his Maker's displeasure—and in a moment of complete desperation he confesses that it has become more than he can bear. With his bones wasting away and all his strength dried up, David realized he could not fight against it any longer.

Note that conviction is also a gracious act of God's mercy. To permit us to sense the wrong we have done, to feel the just weight of God's heavy hand without experiencing simultaneously the just punishment we deserve for our sin is a most lavish demonstration of God's kindness.

It is critical to also point out that while there is a valid Spirit-initiated conviction that will lead a person toward repentance toward God, there is also a counterfeit conviction that will lead a person elsewhere. Listen to Paul's words to the Corinthian church:

> As it is, I rejoice, not because you were grieved, but because you were grieved into repenting. For you felt a godly grief, so that you suffered no loss through us. For godly grief

produces a repentance that leads to salvation without regret, whereas worldly grief produces death. (2 Corinthians 7:9-10)

The 'godly grief' spoken of here is the heart-felt conviction (sorrow and remorse) for the wrong committed against God. Paul is also reminding us that there are people who can experience sorrow for being caught in their wrongdoing, feel really bad about it, and still not repent toward God. 'Worldly grief' will lead a person into denial and misery, away from God and toward death. Having one's wrongdoing exposed only to hastily make the routine promise that it won't ever happen again is not true repentance toward God. Saying or doing whatever is needed merely for sake of not feeling guilty anymore is not genuine conviction.

Humanity's solution to ridding oneself of the piercing sensation of guilt is to attempt to massage it out of one's conscience. Opting to surround ourselves with teachers, counselors, and celebrities who confidently assure us that we are not actually guilty of anything, but instead, only in need of tapping into our true inner-self in order to unleash our potential is spiritual forgery.

Authentic conviction always leads to genuine repentance. Look at David's confession in verse five of Psalm 32:

⁵I acknowledged my sin to you,
     and I did not cover my iniquity;
I said, "I will confess my transgressions to the LORD,"
     and you forgave the iniquity of my sin.

This is an invaluable picture of what genuine repentance is. David, having been unable to stand, now acknowledges his sinful condition before his holy God. He cannot escape this reality. David has concluded there is no place he can go, but toward God:

> Where shall I go from your Spirit?
>> Or where shall I flee from your presence?
> If I ascend to heaven, you are there!
>> If I make my bed in Sheol, you are there!
> If I take the wings of the morning
>> and dwell in the uttermost parts of the sea,
> even there your hand shall lead me,
>> and your right hand shall hold me.
> If I say, "Surely the darkness shall cover me,
>> and the light about me be night,"
> even the darkness is not dark to you;
>> the night is bright as the day,
>> for darkness is as light with you. (Psalm 139:7-12)

In David's moment of true repentance he doesn't attempt to cover his own sin. He doesn't try to run from it, or skirt the issue before him. He doesn't attempt to introduce a watered-down definition of what sin is with the false notion that what he has done is in fact really not to be considered that bad. In another Psalm, David describes the magnitude of sin itself and its devastating effect:

> For I know my transgressions,
>> and my sin is ever before me.
> Against you, you only, have I sinned
>> and done what is evil in your sight,
> so that you may be justified in your words
>> and blameless in your judgment. (Psalm 51:3-4)

Having run out of excuses, David's conviction gives way to repentance. He reflects upon his own spiritual condition in a another Psalm: "The sacrifices of God are a broken spirit; a broken and contrite heart, O God, you will not despise" (Psalm 51:17). David is fully aware that there are no negotiations that can be brought to the table; the only option is complete and unconditional surrender to God.

Know this, God *loves* a repentant heart. For the one who approaches God in humility and brokenness, fully aware of his or her sinful condition and the need to make things right, there is always forgiveness—mercy without measure. This great and mighty Creator is also a kind and compassionate heavenly Father. He will never turn away a truly penitent soul.

And with true repentance always comes genuine transformation. The heart, the mind and the will are all affected. The Bible calls it consecration or holiness. Note how David starts out Psalm 32:

> ¹Blessed is the one whose transgression is forgiven,
>   whose sin is covered.
> ²Blessed is the man against whom the LORD counts no iniquity,
>   and in whose spirit there is no deceit.

That's a wonderful summation of a person who has sincerely repented and apprehends what it means to have received total forgiveness. To know that one's sin has been removed and that God no longer will hold that person accountable for his or her transgressions is a wonderful place in which to find oneself. Notice at the end of verse two it says that the one who is genuinely repentant will possess no deceit in his or her spirit. To put it another way, this type of repentance is authentic; there is nothing false to it, there is nothing misleading, there is nothing to conceal.

Remarkably, the mercy of God doesn't stop here. There is still more good news! Listen to the words of Jesus in Mark 1:

> The time is fulfilled, and the kingdom of God is at hand; *repent and believe in the gospel.* (Mark 1:15b)

Jesus instructs us to first repent, and then to believe in the gospel, otherwise known as the good news. Just what is this good news in which we are told to believe? It is the message that God has secured the required remedy for the removal of the debt he requires for sin itself.

You recall that God, in his exercise of justice, requires that a debt must always be paid, without exception, by anyone who sins against him. And the payment he always requires, as we have seen from his own word, is death:

> The soul who sins shall die. (Ezekiel 18:20a)

This is where the news of God gets really good. *The debt we owe for sin has been paid in full!*

> And you, who were dead in your trespasses and the uncircumcision of your flesh, God made alive together with him, *having forgiven us all our trespasses, by canceling the record of debt that stood against us with its legal demands. This he set aside, nailing it to the cross.* (Colossians 2:13-14)

It was God and God alone, who, because he has loved us with an everlasting love, unhesitatingly sent his son, Jesus Christ, into the world to offer his life as the payment for the debt of our sin. With mankind, this payment would have been impossible. This reality is unfolded before us in a Psalm:

Truly no man can ransom another,
　　or give to God the price of his life,
for the ransom of their life is costly
　　and can never suffice,
that he should live on forever
　　and never see the pit. (Psalm 49:7-9)

Therefore, God chose to do what we could not. This payment—initiated by our merciful God—was set into motion when Jesus descended from heaven, became a man and then successfully lived a perfect life without sin. Only then could Jesus willingly offer up his sinless life to our heavenly Father through his death upon a cross in exchange for the payment of the debt we owed. In other words, Jesus satisfied the payment God required in order for mankind to escape eternal death and thereby receive eternal life. That is, by far, the best news anyone could ever receive!

But God shows his love for us in that while we were still sinners, Christ died for us. (Romans 5:8)

For our sake he made him to be sin who knew no sin, so that in him we might become the righteousness of God. (2 Corinthians 5:21)

In this the love of God was made manifest among us, that God sent his only Son into the world, so that we might live through him. In this is love, not that we have loved God but that he loved us and sent his Son to be the propitiation for our sins. (1 John 4:9-10)

"Thus it is written, that the Christ should suffer and on the third day rise from the dead, and that repentance and forgiveness of sins should be proclaimed in his name" (Luke 24:46-47)

God has chosen to be merciful. He didn't have to do so. The express intent of his kindness toward us has a single purpose . . . God wants to save us from our sin and to give us eternal life. We read Jesus' own words in John 10, known as the Good Shepherd passage, of God's intent for those who choose to repent and believe in the gospel:

> "My sheep hear my voice, and I know them, and they follow me. *I give them eternal life, and they will never perish, and no one will snatch them out of my hand.* My Father, who has given them to me, is greater than all, and no one is able to snatch them out of the Father's hand. I and the Father are one." (John 10:27-30)

You can't get more merciful than that! Therefore, let it be said that this life-altering message of redemption and eternal life arising from the justice and mercy of God is something we can neither afford to ignore nor delay in our response to him.

> For since the message declared by angels proved to be reliable, and every transgression or disobedience received a just retribution, *how shall we escape if we neglect such a great salvation?* It was declared at first by the Lord, and it was attested to us by those who heard, while God also bore witness by signs and wonders and various miracles and by gifts of the Holy Spirit distributed according to his will. (Hebrews 2:2-4)

Recalibration

What we choose to believe about God, about Jesus, and about ourselves will determine where we will spend eternity. The goal of the Bible's message is crystal clear:

> "How I did not shrink from declaring to you anything that was profitable, and teaching you in public and from house to house, *testifying both to Jews and to Greeks of repentance toward God and of faith in our Lord Jesus Christ."* (Acts 20:20-21)

Let's close out this chapter by countering the bad news with the good news:

The Bad News: God has announced that every single person is a sinner. (Romans 3:23)

The Good News: God has declared that forgiveness for sin is possible for the person who repents. (Luke 24:47)

The Bad News: We are not permitted to use our own definition of sin. (Isaiah 5:20)

The Good News: God has told us what sin is and has provided the payment for the debt of sin we owe. (1 John 3:4-5)

The Bad News: All have been born with a sin nature. (Psalm 51:5)

The Good News: A new nature is birthed in the one who repents and believes. (2 Corinthians 5:17)

The Bad News: People die because of sin. (Ezekiel 18:20)

The Good News: Eternal life is the reward for the sons and daughters of God. (1 John 5:11)

The Bad News: Fairness has nothing to do with it. (Romans 9:20)

The Good News: Justice and mercy have everything to do with it. (Isaiah 30:18)

Justice and mercy are intricately woven into the supernatural fabric of God's pattern of redemption for mankind. If we downplay the truth of the justice of God, we will not properly comprehend the place and purpose of his mercy. Instead, we will be tempted to consider his mercy as something we can earn, or perhaps at some ill-conceived level, come to deserve.

> Evil men do not understand justice,
>> but those who seek the LORD understand it completely.
> (Proverbs 28:5)

Before arriving at the place of repentance toward God, the justice of God is upsetting, unnerving, and a significant cause for fear of judgment, as it should be. Warnings from God are to be taken most seriously and acted upon. They exist for a reason.

But after genuine repentance takes place and forgiveness is experienced, the justice of God actually becomes a place of refuge:

As your name, O God,
> so your praise reaches to the ends of the earth.
Your right hand is filled with righteousness.
> *Let Mount Zion be glad!*
Let the daughters of Judah rejoice
> *because of your judgments!* (Psalm 48:10-11)

Knowing that our Maker will *always* make things right—meeting all injustices with perfect justice—standing up for those who are his—is reassuring living in such an unjust world. Having the promise that nothing will ever escape our heavenly Father's watchful eye over us, his children, provides the opportunity for contentment and trust for which we all long.

May we not forget that all that is in existence today is here only because of the mercy of God. In this world's state of persistent rebellion against its Maker, it could be much, much worse than it is. God is withholding worldwide judgment at this moment because he is merciful. His active work of kindness has also placed restraint on this present evil, therefore giving opportunity for the message of repentance toward God and faith in the Lord Jesus Christ to be proclaimed to all men. God desires that we know the truth about his mercy and justice—the certainty of his kindness and severity. Our eternal salvation rests on it.

> Therefore the LORD waits to be gracious to you, and therefore he exalts himself to show mercy to you. For the LORD is a God of justice; blessed are all those who wait for him. (Isaiah 30:18)

Once you were not a people, but now you are God's people; once you had not received mercy, but now you have received mercy. (1 Peter 2:10)

The saying is trustworthy and deserving of full acceptance, that Christ Jesus came into the world to save sinners, of whom I am the foremost. But I received mercy for this reason, that in me, as the foremost, Jesus Christ might display his perfect patience as an example to those who were to believe in him for eternal life. To the King of the ages, immortal, invisible, the only God, be honor and glory forever and ever. Amen. (1 Timothy 1:15-17)

Discussion Questions

1. Why is the *whole counsel of God* such an important concept?

2. Why do people prefer not to hear the truth about God's justice?

3. In your own words, what is true repentance?

4. Why do we have to first repent and then believe in the Gospel?

5. Why must the good news be filtered through the bad news?

Sunrise at Point Imperial - North Rim - Grand Canyon National Park

The secret things belong to the Lord our God, but the things
that are revealed belong to us and to our children forever.

Deuteronomy 29

8

UNMISTAKEABLY MANIFESTED . . .

the mystery revealed

Everything we know about God has come solely from what God has chosen to reveal of himself. It is through his work of revelation—the method of making himself known—from which we learn of the interconnectivity of all things. The purpose of divine disclosure is to induce both a valid identity of, as well as a genuine relationship with, our Creator. God, through the vehicle of revelation, has provided all that is necessary in order that we may know—without question—who he is, and that he is trustworthy in all things said and done.

The Revelation of God in the Physical Universe

The apostle Paul asserts in the book of Romans: "For what *can be known about God is plain to them*, because *God has shown it to them*. For his invisible attributes, namely, his eternal power and divine nature, *have been clearly perceived*, ever since the creation of the world, in the things that have been made" (1:19-20a).

God's creation account was examined in some detail in chapters two, three, and four. Suffice it to say, as the apostle declares, God has made himself evident to all through the vehicle of creation. He alone is the one true God who first created, and now sustains, all things. Some have coined this God's *General or Natural Revelation*, meaning that God is unmistakably sensed and comprehended to a sufficient degree by every person by reason of creation itself.

We are also assured from the text of Romans 1 that, left to ourselves, every single person inhabiting this planet will do everything within his or her own power to ignore the reality of God's existence, even in the face of all the evidence. We are told in Scripture how this unnatural rejection of God originally came about. Our first parents, Adam and Eve, were given a choice to obey or disobey God. They, in pursuit of self-interest, chose to disobey, which placed all of us on the fatal path of disobedience. Along with that inheritance from our first ancestors was born our stubborn attitude to reject the rights of our Creator. Yet in the midst of civilization's unrelenting rebellion, the evidence for God in creation still remains absolute, unmovable, and intact for all to see.

In the end, when all humanity stands before their Creator to give an account for their lives, not a single person will be able to reply with any legitimacy: "I never knew about God." "I didn't see God." "God, you never showed yourself to me." To the contrary, on that Final Day God will present to everyone the irrefutable evidence that he was always there, seen by all; that he could have been truly found if we would have searched for him; that he could have been personally known if we had believed that he existed. We will all face the inescapable reality that a supernatural relationship with our Maker was offered every single day. There will be no valid explanations on that day, just implausible alibis. Listen once again to the apostle Paul's summation of the situation:

> For when Gentiles, who do not have the law, by nature do what the law requires, they are a law to themselves, even though they do not have the law. *They show that the work of the law is written on their hearts, while their conscience also bears witness, and their conflicting thoughts accuse or even excuse them on that day when, according to my gospel, God judges the secrets of men by Christ Jesus.* (Romans 2:14-16)

Possessing this bit of revelation about the actual condition of those to whom we speak is a great help in identifying their reactionary—and at times, even hostile—attitude when it comes to the issue of accountability to God.

The Revelation of God in The Written Word

Although he could have stopped with just the observable evidence of his divine design in creation, God, out of his intentional love, went a step further and chose to speak directly to us through the text of the Holy Bible comprised of sentences and paragraphs, narratives and historical accounts, songs and poetry, as well as letters and prophecy. His objective with the Bible is to be unmistakably recognized as the one true God who is sovereign over all, directing the course of history through the framework of his unalterable plan of redemption.

In John 17, known as Christ's High Priestly Prayer, Jesus prayed for his followers using these words: "Sanctify them in the truth; your word is truth" (v. 17). Here Jesus is declaring aloud for our benefit the certainty that God can be implicitly trusted in all things. There is no hint of falsehood in him. The complete trustworthiness of God is declared in the Scriptures:

> ... for the sake of the faith of God's elect and their knowledge of the truth, which accords with godliness, in hope of eternal life, *which God, who never lies*, promised before the ages began and at the proper time manifested in his word through the preaching with which I have been entrusted. (Titus 1:1b-3a)

> And now, O Lord GOD, you are God, and *your words are true*. (2 Samuel 7:28a)

> *Every word of God proves true*; he is a shield to those who take refuge in him. (Proverbs 30:5)

> The *words of the LORD are pure words*, like silver refined in a furnace on the ground, purified seven times. (Psalm 12:6)

Some have termed the text of the Bible as *God's Special Revelation*, meaning that God took it upon himself to initiate, orchestrate, and guarantee a faithful and true record of his ways for men to hear, read, understand, and obey. Scripture declares that this was accomplished supernaturally through the vehicle of certain men, chosen by God, who were under the guidance and protection of the Spirit of God during the time of writing. Here are two passages that help us appreciate how God achieved this:

> And we have the prophetic word more fully confirmed, to which you will do well to pay attention as to a lamp shining in a dark place, until the day dawns and the morning star rises in your hearts, knowing this first of all, that *no prophecy*

of Scripture comes from someone's own interpretation. For no prophecy was ever produced by the will of man, but men spoke from God as they were carried along by the Holy Spirit. (2 Peter 1:19-21)

All Scripture is breathed out by God and profitable for teaching, for reproof, for correction, and for training in righteousness, that the man of God may be complete, equipped for every good work. (2 Timothy 3:16-17)

This is not intended to be a polemic (active debate) to prove the Bible. There are wonderful and compelling publications available that go into great detail regarding the unity, reliability, and transmission of Scripture. In this book we are continuing to ask:

• What does God want us to know about himself?
• What does God want us to know about his trustworthiness?

This, as noted previously, is a faith journey that we travel. We must come to God believing that he exists and rewards those who seek after him. No doubt, one of God's greatest rewards is the incredible written account of his story.

At this juncture, let's examine three central particulars regarding God's special revelation: the *accuracy, clarity,* and *usefulness* of the Bible. This will greatly aid in our awareness of God's approach to making himself known.

God's Revelation is Accurate

Every story in the Bible; from Adam and Eve to Noah and the Flood; from the Tower of Babel to Moses and the Ten Commandments; from the Walls of Jericho to Elijah's encounter with the prophets of Baal; from the historical birth and gruesome crucifixion of Jesus to his bodily resurrection and ascension to the right hand of the Father; God asserts took place in real time and happened as described in Scripture. From the first word God spoke to the Bible's completion, God has proven irrefutably that he is neither an author of fiction, nor are those whom he chose to pen for him.

Since we believe the story God has chosen to tell us is true, it should not surprise us when we hear some modern-day unbelieving archeologists—much to their chagrin—being duty-bound to confess that after careful investigation of their digs, the biblical accounts once in question are in fact now to be viewed as being historically accurate. For example, having previously thought to be referenced only in the Bible, and thereby bringing into serious question the Bible's reliability, recent archeological discoveries affirming the existence of the people called Hittites, King David, and Pontus Pilate, have served to reinforce the accuracy of the Bible. As Christians who follow the one true God, we should expect nothing less than the truth of God's word to be turning up all around us, even when one chooses to use a brush, shovel, and a pick.

God's recorded acts are more than merely exaggerated stories of naturalistic causes. Still, television shows seem determined to depict the miracles described in the Bible as explainable through nature via fierce winds, destructive volcanoes, and freak storms, mixed with a chance-happening of people being in the right place at the right time. The media-prophets continue to purport that these ancient stories were, in fact, spun hyperbolically around family fires, which in turn, elevated these naturalistic occurrences to the stuff of legends and myths, thus making for a good read in a book like the Bible.

The producers of these types of shows are fully aware that there is an inherent human curiosity with events that seem unexplainable and mysterious, even mystical, and beyond one's comprehension. Knowing that we will carelessly flip the channel to watch shows promising new revelation on the previously unknown, they have capitalized upon our gullibility to explain away God-stories through what they would presume happened by way of a natural coincidence. Unfortunately, few, if any, of these stories allow for the supernatural intervention of a sovereign God.

The apostle John would have a poignant comment or two to make if he were writing in today's culture. Listen to what he wrote some 1900+ years ago: "I write these things to you about *those who are trying to deceive you*. But the anointing that you received from him abides in you, and you have no need that anyone should teach you. But as his anointing teaches you about everything, and *is true, and is no lie*—just as it has taught you, abide in him" (1 John 2:26-27).

One thing of which we can be certain: there is no hidden agenda in the Bible. God has stated with divine exactness who he is, how he wants to be understood, and what he intends to do to bring about a future for his people:

> "I am the LORD; that is my name; my glory I give to no other, nor my praise to carved idols. Behold, *the former things have come to pass, and new things I now declare; before they spring forth I tell you of them.*" (Isaiah 42:8-9)

Our awareness of God's revelatory precision can serve to reinforce our confidence in the trustworthiness of God.

God's Revelation is Clear

> But as for you, continue in what you have learned and have firmly believed, knowing from whom you learned it and how from childhood you have been acquainted with *the sacred writings, which are able to make you wise for salvation through faith in Christ Jesus.* (2 Timothy 3:14-15)

To declare that the Bible's message is clear *does not imply* that it is simplistic. The apostle Peter confesses in 2 Peter 3: "Our beloved brother Paul also wrote to you according to the wisdom given him, as he does in all his letters when he speaks in them of these matters. *There are some things in them that are hard to understand*, which the ignorant and unstable twist to their own destruction, as they do the other Scriptures" (vv. 15b-16). Peter confesses that there are some scriptural passages that his fellow apostle writes that require diligent study. He doesn't say Paul's writing is impossible to comprehend, but that it takes more than just a cursory devotional approach to get at the true meaning.

What is the clear message God wants us to take from the Bible? The apostle John, writing under the direction of the Holy Spirit, gets as close as anyone. 1 John 2 says: "And this is the promise that he made to us—eternal life" (v. 25). God has given us the Bible so we may know how to enter into and experience eternal life with him. The story summarized goes something like this:

• God creates all things supernaturally. (Genesis 1)

• Adam (the representative of all mankind) and Eve rebel, choosing to disobey their Creator and therefore reject God in their life. (Genesis 3:1-19)

164

• God promises that despite mankind's rejection of God, he will still reclaim them. (Isaiah 11:10-16)

• Men and women, in their sinful nature, continue to rebel while God extends an open call for everyone to return to him. (Nehemiah 1:8-10)

• God, at the proper time, sends his Son, Jesus the Christ, in order to reclaim mankind. (1 Timothy 2:5-6)

• Mankind rejects Jesus and puts the Son of God on a cross and kills him. (Matthew 27)

• God demonstrates the futility of mankind's efforts to be rid of God by raising Jesus from the dead on the third day. (Matthew 28:1-10)

• Mankind denies that this ever happened. (Matthew 28:11-15)

• God reveals that this event—the death and resurrection of Jesus—the act that would secure eternal life for men and women—had actually been planned all along. (Luke 24:44-47)

• Men and women were to be given the opportunity to turn away from their rebellion and accept God's remedy for a restored relationship with him. (Hebrews 3:7-14)

• God continues to offer to this very day the free gift of eternal life to any person who will repent of his or her sin and turn to Christ and trust in his finished work. (Romans 10:9-10)

• Men and women have to make a choice, to stay where they are, or make a move toward God. (2 Corinthians 6:2)

• God will not extend this invitation indefinitely. (Revelation 14:14-16)

• Men and women will be held personally responsible if they die while they are in rebellion. (Revelation 20:11-15)

• God will reward those who choose Christ with the gift of life eternal in the New Heavens and the New Earth. (Revelation 21-22)

When we speak of the Bible's message being clear, what we are saying is that any person can read Scripture and can discover what is needed in order to restore their relationship with God. Whether they will choose to act on the words they read and hear, or not, is yet another matter.

What does God want out of all this? He wants a relationship with us. The Bible provides the needed coordinates to find our way back to him. Romans chapter 10 serves as one of those spiritual GPS waymarks for anyone desiring to hear what God requires of his creation: "If you *confess with your mouth* that Jesus is Lord and *believe in your heart* that God raised him from the dead, you will be saved. For with the heart one believes and is justified, and with the mouth one confesses and is saved" (vv. 9-10).

God's Word is clear; the Bible has been placed in our hands as our divine roadmap for eternal life. The Scriptures declare: "And *this is eternal life*, that they know you the only true God, and Jesus Christ whom you have sent" (John 17:3).

God's Revelation is Instructional

> All Scripture is breathed out by God and *profitable for teaching, for reproof, for correction, and for training in righteousness, that the man of God may be complete, equipped for every good work.* (2 Timothy 3:16-17)

The Bible reveals to its readers a plethora of sound, functional, hands-on tools for successful everyday living. Here are three to consider:

1. *God has revealed how he wants us to live.* Our Maker does not intend for us to wander through this life trying to figure out how to best make things work, whether it be through the process of elimination or our best educated guess, although this is the state in which many who occupy our modern churches find themselves. In fact, our heavenly Father has removed a lot of the guesswork out of living. He has told us *how we can live* in order to get the most out of life:

> And whatever you do, in word or deed, do everything in the name of the Lord Jesus, giving thanks to God the Father through him. (Colossians 3:17)

> So, whether you eat or drink, or whatever you do, do all to the glory of God. (1 Corinthians 10:31)

> Whatever you do, work heartily, as for the Lord and not for men, knowing that from the Lord you will receive the inheritance as your reward. You are serving the Lord Christ. (Colossians 3:23-24)

As obedient children, do not be conformed to the passions of your former ignorance, but as he who called you is holy, you also be holy in all your conduct, since it is written, "You shall be holy, for I am holy." (1 Peter 1:14-16)

But the fruit of the Spirit is love, joy, peace, patience, kindness, goodness, faithfulness, gentleness, self-control; against such things there is no law. (Galatians 5:22-23)

2. *God has revealed how he wants us to worship.* Our Creator understands that every person possesses an innate desire to worship and adore someone or something. It is in our spiritual makeup to do so. It is how he fashioned us. That being a reality, God does not want us to miss our opportunity to find true significance in that process. Our Maker has revealed that we have been created to worship him; it is only in the realm of worship where we will find our truest sense of our reason for being.

"You shall have no other gods before me." (Exodus 20:3)

Ascribe to the LORD the glory due his name; bring an offering and come before him! Worship the LORD in the splendor of holiness. (1 Chronicles 16:29)

Oh come, let us worship and bow down; let us kneel before the LORD, our Maker! (Psalm 95:6)

Exalt the LORD our God; worship at his footstool! Holy is he! (Psalm 99:5)

"But the hour is coming, and is now here, when the true worshipers will worship the Father in spirit and truth, for the Father is seeking such people to worship him." (John 4:23)

I appeal to you therefore, brothers, by the mercies of God, to present your bodies as a living sacrifice, holy and acceptable to God, which is your spiritual worship. (Romans 12:1)

… not neglecting to meet together, as is the habit of some, but encouraging one another, and all the more as you see the Day drawing near. (Hebrews 10:25)

3. *God has revealed how he wants us to interrelate.* This planet is teeming with humanity. Unfortunately, it is an observable reality that not all of us get along. This is the evidence of man's rebellion against God. Man wants to be left alone to do his own thing. He doesn't want to be bothered by others. He doesn't want accountability to anyone or anything. Yet our Creator knows that despite mankind's insistence to be left alone, men and women are still social creatures in need of relationship. In his infinite wisdom found throughout Scripture, God has provided the keys for maintaining authentic relationships:

"A new commandment I give to you, that you love one another: just as I have loved you, you also are to love one another." (John 13:34)

Love one another with brotherly affection. Outdo one another in showing honor. (Romans 12:10)

Owe no one anything, except to love each other, for the one who loves another has fulfilled the law. (Romans 13:8)

For you were called to freedom, brothers. Only do not use your freedom as an opportunity for the flesh, but through love serve one another. (Galatians 5:13)

And let us consider how to stir up one another to love and good works, (Hebrews 10:24)

Above all, keep loving one another earnestly, since love covers a multitude of sins. (1 Peter 4:8)

Do nothing from selfish ambition or conceit, but in humility count others more significant than yourselves. Let each of you look not only to his own interests, but also to the interests of others. (Philippians 2:3-4)

Just from these few selected passages of Scripture, it is clear that our heavenly Father has revealed a very practical approach for his sons and daughters to experience an abundant life every single day.

Recalibration

The world doesn't like the Christian's view of the Bible—the belief that the Bible is God's factual record of man's history, the description of God's direct intervention, and the divine prescription for every person's future. Our culture would prefer to continue downgrading the Bible as irrelevant, relegating it to the halls of liberal proponents of higher criticism, skeptical linguists, and unbelieving professors.

While scientific and historical accuracy is helpful to affirm the truthfulness of the biblical record, for the Christian, the Bible serves a much more central purpose as we see in the text of Hebrews:

For *the word of God is living and active*, sharper than any two-edged sword, piercing to the division of soul and of spirit, of joints and of marrow, and *discerning the thoughts and intentions of the heart.* (Hebrews 4:12)

The Bible is more than mere words on a page. It is alive and operational. It declares of itself that it is an invincible offensive weapon. The truth of the Bible is able to penetrate without resistance, thereby exposing every man and woman to his or her own true spiritual condition. The Word of God searches the motives and ambitions of the heart, ferreting out what is true and right, and what is false and immoral. It doesn't miss a thing. The Word of God looks under every rock, peers into every crevice, and knows what is behind every locked door of the heart. That is why the world does not like the Christian's view of the Bible. The truth of the matter is that every single man and woman outside of God prefers his or her own darkness to God's light of revelation:

"And this is the judgment: the light has come into the world, and *people loved the darkness rather than the light* because their works were evil. For everyone who does wicked things hates the light and does not come to the light, lest his works should be exposed. But whoever does what is true comes to the light, so that it may be clearly seen that his works have been carried out in God." (John 3:19-21)

Humanity does not want light to shine into their lives, for it would reveal a very different perspective—a way of life to which they are not accustomed. The nominal Christian is often conflicted here as well, knowing he or she should be walking in the light, but for lack of discipline and/or his or her insistence on privacy finds himself or herself also lurking in the shadows.

It is evident that the world has rejected the truth in the Bible and in creation. Nevertheless, God assures us that his light of revelation—despite the opposition—will continue to shine brightly for all to see and believe until the Final Day. And we have the guarantee from Scripture that while many men and women will choose to run from the light, there will be those who will in fact accept our invitation to step out into the radiance of God's glorious salvation. No longer will that person need to feel his or her way through this life, stumbling over his or her own disobedience. Jesus' own words promise this very thing:

> Again Jesus spoke to them, saying, "I am the light of the world. Whoever follows me will not walk in darkness, but will have the light of life." (John 8:12)

Discussion Questions

1. Why do people so confidently deny God's existence?

2. How does creation serve as a part of God's revelation?

3. Why is the accuracy of Scripture in all things imperative?

4. How does the Bible serve as a tool for the Gospel message?

5. Why does the Bible encourage community over individualism?

Clear Creek Falls - Creede, Colorado

These things God has revealed to us through the Spirit.
For the Spirit searches everything, even the depths of God.

1 Corinthians 2

9

THE SPIRIT WITHOUT MEASURE . . .

He will teach you all things

The Holy Spirit is the indispensable component for anyone who would desire to understand what God is saying. Without the Spirit's supernatural work of illumination in a person's heart and mind, God's Word, although wholly true, will remain in fact, only words; text will remain only text; and stories will remain only stories. The apostle Paul puts it this way:

> *Now we have received not the spirit of the world, but the Spirit who is from God, that we might understand the things freely given us by God.* And we impart this in words not taught by human wisdom but taught by the Spirit, interpreting spiritual truths to those who are spiritual. *The natural person does not accept the things of the Spirit of God,* for they are folly to him, and *he is not able to understand them because they are spiritually discerned.* (1 Corinthians 2:12-14)

The natural person spoken of here is brought into direct contrast with the spiritual person. The natural person is under the influence of the godless spirit of the world; the spiritual person is under the influence of the Spirit of God. The natural person comprehends life only from a worldly point of view; the spiritual person, being a partaker of the divine nature (2 Peter 1:3-4), is able to understand the things of God through the Spirit. The natural person is a stranger to God; the spiritual person is a follower of God.

Paul's intention is to remind his readers that it is impossible for anyone to truly know God and what he is doing devoid of the Spirit's presence in one's life. Without the Holy Spirit's work of illumination in a person, belief in God will continually be perceived as silly and make-believe. The dismissive attitude of 'natural man' toward his Creator will most assuredly remain . . . unless something supernaturally transpires.

The Spirit of God makes it possible for a person to understand, speak, and act in a manner pleasing to the Father. Did you know that an individual cannot begin to know and experience God unless the Spirit first determines to initiate a work in his or her life? Let's examine some of the evidence of the Spirit's sovereign work in our lives.

The Capacity to Understand

The disciples spent three years listening to—and being personally trained by—the Lord Jesus. Anyone who spends three years working on a degree can, at the end of their coursework, be expected to have a decent grasp on the particular discipline they have studied. It is also assumed that after devoting one's self to three years of training, a person is going to be able to use what they have learned with a certain level of expertise in order to be able to go out and earn a living.

Do not overlook the fact that the disciples didn't just attend classes two or three times a week like those in a degree program. No, the disciples were with Jesus 24/7 365 days a year. They walked with him, they prayed with him, they listened to his every word, they shared every meal with him, and they slept alongside him. Rarely leaving his side, they witnessed in minute detail how he conducted himself in the affairs of everyday life. Yet despite this extended 'on the job training,' we discover that the disciples were still unable to comprehend what was really needed in order to make sense of this new life and to carry out the responsibilities he was passing on to them.

The inability to 'connect the dots' in life leaves a person spending much of their time guessing what to do or think. We see this dynamic going on in the disciples' lives for those three years. Again and again Jesus would ask them questions like: "Where is your faith?" "Have you not heard?" "Don't you remember?" "Who do you say that I am?" By repeatedly asking such questions, Christ was actually revealing to them a deficiency, letting his followers feel the gravity that apart from the Spirit of God, they could not apprehend what was happening around them and the role they were being asked to assume.

But Jesus didn't stop with the revelation that what the disciples knew was in fact wholly insufficient; out of sheer love for his followers, Christ reached out supernaturally with the divine remedy for their inability to understand. We see this played out in Luke 24. In the context, Jesus has been raised bodily from the dead; the disciples, unaware of the resurrection, are now in hiding. Distraught over what they had just experienced—the murder of their Master—they find themselves mulling over the prospects of making a clean getaway:

> As they were talking about these things, Jesus himself stood among them, and said to them, "Peace to you!" But they were startled and frightened and thought they saw a spirit. And he said to them, "Why are you troubled, and why do doubts arise in your hearts? See my hands and my feet, that it is I myself. Touch me, and see. For a spirit does not have flesh and bones as you see that I have." And when he had said this, he showed them his hands and his feet. And while they still disbelieved for joy and were marveling, he said to them, "Have you anything here to eat?" They gave him a piece of broiled fish, and he took it and ate before them. Then he said to them, "These are my words that I spoke to you while I was still with you, that everything written about me in the law of Moses and the Prophets and the Psalms must be fulfilled." *Then he opened their minds to understand the Scriptures*, and said to them, "Thus it is written, that the Christ should suffer and on the third day rise from the dead, and that repentance and forgiveness of sins should be proclaimed in his name to all nations, beginning from Jerusalem."(Luke 24:36-47)

We observe in this text that for the first time in the three-plus years the disciples were given a gift from Jesus none of them had received up to that point. Jesus gave them *the capacity to understand.* All that they had previously heard and learned from him they now began to comprehend supernaturally. They could put two and two together. At last, they were able to connect the dots and to see things as they really were. Sorrow was turned to joy. Fear was turned to confidence. Darkness gave way to the Light. The Holy Spirit, in an instant, literally transformed their thought processes, both in their perceptions and their ability to recall. Their memories now meant something. They understood, as they never had before. They now *knew*.

Like those followers in the first century, we, too, can listen Sunday after Sunday, and still never apprehend the truth, that is until God sovereignly chooses to unveil it. Our own cognitive prowess does not give us an inroad to knowing God. The fact is that not a single one of us possesses the capacity to understand as we should, until God, in his gracious act of mercy, gives us the Spirit.

Interestingly, the apostle John describes the very same event in his Gospel account; although, he uses different terminology. Listen to John in chapter 20:

> On the evening of that day, the first day of the week, the doors being locked where the disciples were for fear of the Jews, Jesus came and stood among them and said to them, "Peace be with you." When he had said this, he showed them his hands and his side. Then the disciples were glad when they saw the Lord. Jesus said to them again, "Peace be with you. As the Father has sent me, (even so I am sending you." And when he had said this, *he breathed on them and said to them, "Receive the Holy Spirit."* (John 20:19-22)

Jesus' opening the disciples' minds to understand the Scriptures in Luke 24 and Jesus' breathing on them and saying: "Receive the Holy Spirit," in John 20, both are depicting the same event. Jesus is imparting the Holy Spirit for true spiritual knowledge and insight.

These recorded events can help us better grasp Paul's statement that apart from the Spirit of God making things known, we cannot know as we ought. The Holy Spirit is the only person who can give us the capacity to truly understand.

The Faith to Believe

Here is a spiritual gem; our faith is also a gift from God. The act of imparting faith to us is the supernatural work of the Holy Spirit, born out of love, in order that we may turn to and believe in the one true God. Left to ourselves, we won't yield to the command to forsake all and follow him. We aren't the least bit interested in doing that on our own. The Bible is quite clear; there is not a single person on this earth who will seek after God voluntarily. Listen to Paul's declaration in Romans 3: "None is righteous, no, not one; no one understands; *no one seeks for God.* All have turned aside; together they have become worthless; no one does good, not even one" (vv. 10-12).

Knowing the true human condition makes Ephesians 2:8-9 all the more powerful:

> For by grace you have been saved through faith. And this is not your own doing; *it is the gift of God,* not a result of works, so that no one may boast. (Ephesians 2:8-9)

The salvation that we personally experience arises from the reservoir of God's own grace and is planted in our hearts via the vehicle of faith which Paul assures us is also a gift. The biblical writers are intent to cut the legs out from under our egos, removing all possibility for boasting, as if we were really able to somehow aid in God's supernatural work of salvation. Since God assures us that we can't contribute anything to it, we dare not claim any of the credit for it. That would be spiritual plagiarism.

God sovereignly accomplished all that is needed through the work of his Son Jesus for us to be restored to a right and proper relationship with him. It is both a marvelous and humbling thing to discover that our own personal sense of desiring to know God, to pursue him, and discover what he is about, is a sure sign that the Spirit of God is already actively at work in us.

The Ability to Obey

Our Creator has made it clear what he wants out of our lives. Our Heavenly Father desires willing obedience from us, done for the right reasons, based upon right motives. But the Bible also reminds us of the truth that left in our current condition, without God's intervention, we are never going to choose to do the right things for the right reasons. The prophet Jeremiah declares: "Can the Ethiopian change his skin or the leopard his spots? *Then also you can do good who are accustomed to do evil.*" (13:23). Listen to Paul's summation in Romans:

> For those who live according to the flesh set their minds on the things of the flesh, but those who live according to the Spirit set their minds on the things of the Spirit. For to set the mind on the flesh is death, but to set the mind on the Spirit is life and peace. *For the mind that is set on the flesh is hostile to God, for it does not submit to God's law; indeed, it cannot. Those who are in the flesh cannot please God.*

> You, however, are not in the flesh but in the Spirit, if in fact the Spirit of God dwells in you. Anyone who does not have the Spirit of Christ does not belong to him. But if Christ is in you, although the body is dead because of sin, the Spirit is life because of righteousness. (Romans 8:5-10)

To be sure, left to our own efforts, we won't do that which is truly good because, as the Bible discloses, we are not able to do so. Our daily choices reveal this, telling on us again and again. In our own environment our motives are not pure. We choose to act based on self-interest, self-preservation, and recognition. Even our best efforts don't catch God's eye. Listen to his prophet, Isaiah: "*All our righteous deeds* are like a polluted garment" (Isaiah 64:6b).

So how does our obedience become something that is pleasing to God? If our best efforts don't cut it, what are we supposed to do? This is the beauty of an all-powerful Creator. God, out of his tender mercy and grace, knowing that true obedience can only arise out of a heart for him, and knowing that man, left to himself, does not have a heart for God, stepped in and performed a supernatural miracle:

> "I will sprinkle clean water on you, and you shall be clean from all your uncleannesses, and from all your idols I will cleanse you. And *I will give you a new heart, and a new spirit I will put within you.* And I will remove the heart of stone from your flesh and *give you a heart of flesh.* And *I will put my Spirit within you*, and *cause you to walk* in my statutes and be careful *to obey my rules.*" (Ezekiel 36:25-27)

Our Creator has assured us that we can truly have a heart for him. But in order to accomplish that, he will have to perform some serious surgery. God knew that for true obedience to be possible in our lives, it would take more than mere commands for moral reformation; it would necessitate complete spiritual regeneration from within; a heart transplant of the truest sort. The post-surgical prognosis, God informs us, is that his Spirit will be put within us and the he will cause us to walk in true obedience. Now that is radical surgery!

Here are several verses to consider that detail the type of obedience God is after as it relates to our relationship with him:

With what shall I come before the LORD, and bow myself before God on high? Shall I come before him with burnt offerings, with calves a year old? Will the LORD be pleased with thousands of rams, with ten thousands of rivers of oil? Shall I give my firstborn for my transgression, the fruit of my body for the sin of my soul? *He has told you, O man, what is good; and what does the LORD require of you but to do justice, and to love kindness, and to walk humbly with your God?* (Micah 6:6-8)

"What to me is the multitude of your sacrifices? says the LORD; I have had enough of burnt offerings of rams and the fat of well-fed beasts; I do not delight in the blood of bulls, or of lambs, or of goats. When you come to appear before me, who has required of you this trampling of my courts? Bring no more vain offerings; incense is an abomination to me. New moon and Sabbath and the calling of convocations—I cannot endure iniquity and solemn assembly. Your new moons and your appointed feasts my soul hates; they have become a burden to me; I am weary of bearing them. When you spread out your hands, I will hide my eyes from you; even though you make many prayers, I will not listen; your hands are full of blood. Wash yourselves; make yourselves clean, remove the evil of your deeds from before my eyes; *cease to do evil, learn to do good; seek justice, correct oppression; bring justice to the fatherless, plead the widow's cause."* (Isaiah 1:11-17)

But the *fruit of the Spirit is love, joy, peace, patience, kindness, goodness, faithfulness, gentleness, self-control*; against such things there is no law. (Galatians 5:22-23)

The ability to obey God's commands from a sincere heart (one that is humble and contrite) is evidence that the Spirit has empowered you. Jesus declared to us that apart from him, we could do nothing. If the fruit of obedience is present in your life, the Holy Spirit is at work. Note this type of fruit cannot be self-produced. At best, we might be able to fool a few people with some imitation wax fruit, but as the day heats up and a bite is eventually taken out of our lives, it will be exposed for what it truly is.

So how do I know if I am truly obeying God in a manner pleasing to him? That you would even want to obey your Creator is a very good sign that God is actively at work in you. Paul described it this way: "Therefore, my beloved, as you have always obeyed, so now, not only as in my presence but much more in my absence, work out your own salvation with fear and trembling, for it is *God who works in you, both to will and to work for his good pleasure*" (Philippians 2:12-13).

Make no mistake, you will not ask for that which you do not want. Desiring God indicates he has shown you the path to life. For the one whom God has transformed from within there will be a passion to pursue and a yearning to obey. For this person, the Lord's call found in Jeremiah 6 is doable:

Thus says the LORD: "Stand by the roads, and look, and ask for the ancient paths, where the good way is; and walk in it, and find rest for your souls." (Jeremiah 6:16a)

The Power to Declare

Jesus knew exactly what the disciples would need in order to effectively carry on his message as he himself prepared to return to the Father. Luke 24 says: "You are witnesses of these things. And behold, I am sending the promise of my Father upon you. But *stay in the city until you are clothed with power from on high*" (vv. 48-49). And again, Jesus tells his followers in Acts 1: "But *you will receive power when the Holy Spirit has come upon you*, and you will be my witnesses in Jerusalem and in all Judea and Samaria, and to the end of the earth" (v. 8).

The resurrected Jesus instructed his disciples to use everything they would say and do in life as a witness to what had happened in Jerusalem. He went a step further, telling them that they would be commissioned as the first ones to take this salvation story beyond the city walls into the rest of the world. But in order to do that, they would need supernatural power. The boldness that would be required to stand against the authorities of this world, and to call men and women to a denial of self, challenging them to yield to their Creator would take much more than just a nice homily or two.

So Jesus told his disciples to wait. Typically, our first inclination would be to hit the street or the supermarket telling everyone who would listen that we had just seen a resurrected body with our own eyes. The disciples were different now. They hadn't been the same since Jesus had opened their minds to understand the Scriptures (Luke 24). This time around they were able to connect the dots of God's redemptive story.

With newfound power to obey, they headed for the Upper Room in Jerusalem and waited. The disciples now trusted Jesus implicitly. He had told them that it was necessary that he leave them in order that the Comforter could come. The Comforter, which is the Spirit of God, would teach them all things. The Holy Spirit would use their memories to bring to mind the proper words to speak that could bring life to the hearers. The Holy Spirit would convict the world of sin, righteousness, and judgment. The Holy Spirit would bear witness incessantly of the work and person of Jesus himself. And finally, the Holy Spirit would distribute spiritual gifts to each believer in order to build up the church.

As the account unfolds in Acts, we see that the disciples were in fact clothed with power from on high. They were supernaturally filled with the Holy Spirit, just as Jesus said it would happen, and from that point forward, they never looked back. Here are just a couple of instances from the book of Acts depicting their newfound power:

> Now when they saw *the boldness of Peter and John*, and perceived that they were uneducated, common men, they were astonished. And they recognized that they had been with Jesus. (Acts 4:13)

> "And now, Lord, look upon their threats and grant to your servants to continue to *speak your word with all boldness*, while you stretch out your hand to heal, and signs and wonders are performed through the name of your holy servant Jesus." And when they had prayed, the place in which they were gathered together was shaken, and they were all filled with the Holy Spirit and *continued to speak the word of God with boldness*. (Acts 4:29-31)

> He lived there two whole years at his own expense, and welcomed all who came to him, *proclaiming the kingdom of God*

THE SPIRIT WITHOUT MEASURE

and teaching about the Lord Jesus Christ with all boldness and without hindrance. (Acts 28:30-31)

Jesus commissioned his followers to take his message of salvation into an openly hostile environment, something no normal human being would really want to do—unless they had been changed from within. With the disciples immersed in the power of the Spirit of God, you see a different person. No longer fearful. No longer hesitant. Paul seemed to describe it best when he declares under the authority of the Spirit: "For *God gave us a Spirit* not of fear but *of power and love and self-control*" (2 Timothy 1:7).

The story the disciples testified to in the first century is our story today. The assignment Jesus gave them is our assignment. The responsibility hasn't changed; except that perhaps the message of salvation should become more urgently shared with more boldness as we draw closer to the visible return of Jesus.

It is assuring to know that the same resurrection power and supernatural boldness displayed in the early church is ours to experience also, because we have been given the same Spirit. God has promised in his Word that he will continue to pour out his Spirit in the same fashion as he did in the first century until his Son returns in the clouds for all to see:

> *"And in the last days it shall be,"* God declares, *"that I will pour out my Spirit on all flesh,* and your sons and your daughters shall prophesy, and your young men shall see visions, and your old men shall dream dreams; even on my male servants and female servants in those days *I will pour out my Spirit,* and they shall prophesy. And I will show wonders in the heavens above and signs on the earth below, blood, and fire, and vapor of smoke; the sun shall be turned to darkness and the

moon to blood, before the day of the Lord comes, the great and magnificent day. *And it shall come to pass that everyone who calls upon the name of the Lord shall be saved.*" (Acts 2:17-21 cf. Joel 2:28-32)

While we possess this power from the Spirit of God to declare the mighty works of God, we must be mindful of our need to faithfully study and know God's story through the filter of the Holy Spirit's tutelage. We don't stop thinking or reading when we choose to follow Christ, but instead, we are instructed to submit our minds daily to the Spirit's formation and transformation (Romans 12:1-3). When one speaks from a transformed mind and a heart yielded to the Spirit's prompting, supernatural things will happen. The message God expects us to speak forth to the world does not rest upon cleverly crafted man-oriented sentences and arguments, but instead, our words come in the demonstration of the Spirit and of power (1 Corinthians 2:4-5).

The apostle Paul reminds us that our assignment from God is somewhat simple and straightforward; as representatives of God, we have the responsibility of faithfully planting and watering, believing that the message we speak will not be in vain, but that God will sovereignly have his way:

What then is Apollos? What is Paul? Servants through whom you believed, as the Lord assigned to each. *I planted, Apollos watered, but God gave the growth.* So neither he who plants nor he who waters is anything, but only God who gives the growth. He who plants and he who waters are one, and each will receive his wages according to his labor. (1 Corinthians 3:5-8)

God asks us to be faithful in the tasks he gives us. He promises that in our yieldedness to him, the Spirit's power will be there. By his Spirit we can know, we can believe, we can obey, and we can declare. All thanks will continually flow to God for his miraculous work through his Spirit's transforming presence in our lives.

Recalibration

While it is imperative that we speak the truth of the Bible, it is only the Spirit of God that can give a person true understanding. Unless the Spirit chooses to remove the scales from the eyes, man will remain spiritually blind, unable to see God truly:

> And even if our gospel is veiled, it is veiled to those who are perishing. In their case the *god of this world has blinded the minds of the unbelievers*, to keep them from seeing the light of the gospel of the glory of Christ, who is the image of God. (2 Corinthians 4:3-4)

In the same manner, unless the Spirit of God chooses to remove the veil over the heart, man will remain untouched, continually reading, always listening, but never really understanding or knowing:

> *But their minds were hardened.* For to this day, when they read the old covenant, that same veil remains unlifted, because only through Christ is it taken away. Yes, to this day whenever Moses is read *a veil lies over their hearts.* But *when one turns to the Lord, the veil is removed.* Now the Lord is the Spirit, and *where the Spirit of the Lord is, there is freedom.* (2 Corinthians 3:14-17)

Man's spiritual blindness and hardness of heart should concern us in the same way it concerns God. If we remain untouched, unmoved to pray or to get involved, that too, should be cause for concern. God has given us the tremendous responsibility and privilege of putting the truth on display. Our life in the Spirit is to remove all doubt before the world that God is who he says he is. We are to live transparently, peacefully, powerfully, and without apology. We are to pray hard, pursue understanding, and be ready at any moment to move, all in the power of the Spirit.

Life in the Spirit is neither foolish, nor are the things of God silly, as our culture would taunt. A Spirit-filled life in Christ is a supernatural gift from God so that we may have eternal life. This inestimable generosity from our heavenly Father is what makes our relationship him a reality. The Spirit of God fuels our passion to pursue him, turning our hearts and minds away from the things of this world and toward the things of God.

> Or do you not know that *your body is a temple of the Holy Spirit* within you, whom you have from God? You are not your own, for you were bought with a price. *So glorify God in your body*. (1 Corinthians 6:19-20)

Discussion Questions

1. Why is the Spirit of God indispensable?

2. Why does the world consider God silly and make-believe?

3. What is the Spirit's role in our receiving eternal life?

4. What is the evidence of the activity of the Spirit at work today?

5. How does understanding the Spirit's role in God's plan of redemption assist us in our efforts to share our faith?

Springtime! - Sonoran Desert - Arizona

The grass withers, the flower fades,
but the word of our God will stand forever.

Isaiah 40

10

MORE THAN JUST AN OPINION . . .

each one should be fully convinced

Weeds can be downright deceiving at times. They appear in all shapes and sizes. Some are so attractive that the untrained eye can mistake them as a part of the garden amongst the true flowers. We know that weeds, if not identified and quickly eradicated, can overtake and smother the resident botany. That is why the 'act' of gardening is so critical. Persistent care and oversight ensures an uninhibited bloom to be enjoyed by the senses.

Like a botanical garden, truth holds its own colorful paradise of flavor and color: "Oh, *taste and see* that the LORD is good!" (Psalm 34:8a). Tragically, over the last century, resident caretakers of truth have ignored the seemingly harmless introduction of certain similar-looking weeds, thus permitting them to germinate. These imposters have now begun to thrive as rivals to the real thing. The negligence on the part of truth-cultivators now makes it extremely difficult to distinguish what is really true from the charlatans in our global garden.

Let's look at it another way. We no longer live in a society of mutually understood words. Because of the introduction of the weeds of relativism, situational ethics, and pluralism, we have been pressed into a lifestyle of defining. We must accept our place in this new standard of living, contending for uniform definition, if we are going to speak and convey what we really mean.

For instance, the word *God* is no longer a universally defined and understood word, having been snatched and redefined by modern god-makers. The word God now requires definition, clarification, and description. Thus we use qualifiers such as the *one true* God or *Creator* God. And the challenge isn't just with the word God. Other words, such as *morality, sin, grace,* and *love* as well as the word *truth* itself have been culturally hijacked and are no longer universally understood to mean the same thing they did one hundred years ago. We can no longer assume a person properly understands us when we speak about such things.

Being forced into this brave new world of speaking by definition can be frustrating and even problematic for some Christians. They perceive the chore of having to regularly define what one says about God as tedious, daunting, and exhausting, not to mention that having to add meaning to our words can take up a lot of our valuable time.

We cannot escape the fact that as a participant of humanity we will continue to use words to communicate with each other. It is up to us to decide how we will use our words in conversation. We do have a choice.

Choice #1 - We can continue to freely exchange the culturally universal god-words without clarification. We can let the person listening to us have the freedom to attach their own personal definition and understanding to our words.

Result - They will exit the conversation unchallenged in their thinking and their assumptions. By our not taking the time to communicate clearly and definitively, they take for granted that they have the personal right to keep their own version of god—or no god—intact.

Choice #2 - We can make up a new vocabulary of god-words. Like a secret code, we can use spiritually exotic words and phrases that will quickly classify us as a god-person.

Result - Although unable to comprehend our terminology, he or she will at least sense our efforts to be different. We can also be assured that this person will leave our conversation confused, bewildered, and even intimidated by our vocabulary. Our opting to introduce our own spirit-lingo into the chat builds an uncalled-for barrier between them and us. This unfamiliar speech can leave the impression that we want them to believe we are, in some way, superior to them . . . that we are unchallengeable, and that unless they can learn our speech patterns and begin to mirror our talk, there is little hope for them to find our God.

Choice #3 - We can discipline ourselves to learn to speak clearly by definition, using the words we all use. Terms such as *God, truth,* and *morals* all deserve much more than a passing utterance. They are words packed with definitive meaning and should be recaptured for their intended use.

Result - Although a person may not always agree with us, being confronted with a true definition of God, truth, and morality will challenge their manner of thinking and their personal assumptions.

God's desire is that we truthfully present him in a gentle and kind, yet bold and fearless fashion. Being equipped with authentic meaning affords the Christian a tremendous advantage and gives him or her great hope for every conversation. He or she can confidently speak the truth that God has revealed to all men. However, it will take time to recover and recalibrate our basic understanding of these words.

Seize the Day

Admittedly, God maintains some weighty truth claims:

- He is the one true God. There is no other.
- He is eternal, self-existent and unchangeable.
- He exists as the triune Godhead, one God, in three Persons.
- He created all things, including mankind, through speaking things into existence out of nothing.
- He alone holds together and sustains all things.
- He is holy. His holiness reflects his being transcendent, set apart from all else and morally pure in all facets.
- He has lavished an unconditional love upon his sons and daughters. His love is described as intimate, intentional and indestructible.
- He is full of justice and mercy. Eternal ramifications are attached to his kindness and severity; therefore they are to be carefully considered.
- He has supernaturally revealed to men and women all that they need to know and believe in order to receive eternal life.

• The Spirit of God is essential to knowing God. The Spirit helps and comforts those who are his, bears witness to Christ, and convicts the world of sin, righteousness, and judgment.

There are those today who will openly discredit these claims of God, believing them to be fictitious musings arising out of man's insistence to have god and religion in his life. They prefer to avow that all we really have before us is the evolutionary struggle, i.e., the survival of the fittest. They choose to put their faith in the notion that our existence owes itself to the extraordinary advancement of evolution through the vehicle of chance + time.

Is this assertion of evolutionary certainty merely a personal smokescreen, attempting to make things so hazy that it would be considered fruitless to continue the discussion? Is it an illusion of carnival-like mirrors, with the self-made barker declaring that one's existence is really only what a person makes it? Are they murmuring under their breath: "Back off!"? Are they evolutionary bullies trying to intimidate you by kicking intellectual sand in your eyes, thus imposing a sense that their view is unchallengeable? Is it just a simple "No thanks" to what you believe? Regardless of the initial motivation of the person, you are being afforded a wonderful opportunity to introduce them to the Giver of all life.

Regarding the origin of life, it is crucial to understand that these two statements—creation and evolution—cannot be true at the same time. Either God has told the truth and thus evolution is false, or evolution is true and therefore God is false. A Christian's inattentiveness to these faith collisions at conversational intersections can produce disastrous consequences. We have been entrusted with our Creator's reputation before a watching world. An accurate representation and portrayal of the one true God is what he is after.

At this point in the conversation, predictability comes into play, which provides us an opportunity to position ourselves to be used of God. When a person is reluctant to discuss or consider the assertions God has made about himself, they will reveal one of two mindsets from which they are attempting to defend their life view. One is a mindset of contradiction and the other is a mindset of opposition. Let's briefly have a look at each of these.

The Impossibility of Contradiction

How many times have you heard this statement sermonized in your conversations: "What you choose to believe about the existence of God and the creation of the world is okay for you, but it is not for me. Personally, I choose to believe in evolution."

Examining this assertion closely, we see that a contradiction has been presented. The incompatibility in this method of reasoning is found in the notion that it would be acceptable for one person to hold a particular view, while the other may choose to hold to an opposing view and that they both could be right. This is a problem. Both views cannot be true at the same time. That would be a contradiction.

As human beings we were not created to communicate in contradiction. A contradiction cannot be understood. It is nonsensical and therefore must be rejected. When contradictory declarations such as this arise in our conversations, they must be exposed for what they are, incomprehensible. You do this, not by embarrassing them, but instead, with an honest and sincere offer to journey with them to the conclusion of their contradictory statement. Even if they refuse to agree with your view, they need to recognize the importance of consistency and unity in their own thought processes. God is neither a God of confusion, nor of contradiction. It is our responsibility to expose the fallacy of contradictory thinking in one's belief system. There cannot be God and no God at the same time. That is irrational.

Thinking Christians should not be too taken aback to hear such unsound talk in this day and age. People all around us seem spellbound under the sway of this culture's groundless approach to thinking and reasoning. The false notion of the possibility of subjective truth is pretty much standard fare in our society. It is when a person assumes they can communicate through contradiction that we can address the necessity of understanding what is really true.

The Possibility of Opposition

When exposing a contradiction, note that what is *not* being said is that a person may not hold a different view from what you believe. A man or woman who does not know God, can and often will, hold an opposing view from one who does. Scripturally speaking, this is to be expected. Although opposing views are acceptable in the arena of understanding one another, we must insist that both views cannot be true. Either God is real or there is no God.

The idea that we can meet another somewhere in the middle, with the 'I'm okay, you're okay' subjective approach to a relationship doesn't hold up when it comes to the existence of the one true God. One person is right. The other person is wrong.

Fortunately God has provided the background on why men and women seem to be so opposed to the God of the Bible. The Scripture tells us that there is no one who seeks after God (Romans 3:11). Romans 1 explains the reality that men and women, left to their own imaginations, will make every attempt to suppress the truth of God and his existence. All humanity has chosen to rebel against God and everything connected to him as our Maker, including truth. If given the opportunity, mankind will oppose God on every street corner. It is clear; God is not wanted. But, despite a person's persistent pledge of denial, he or she cannot escape the truth that God is indispensible in this life. Therefore, it is our charge to present the evidence for God that men and women so desperately need. We do this through clear, but gentle, articulation and definition:

> Have no fear of them, nor be troubled, but in your hearts honor Christ the Lord as holy, *always being prepared to make a defense to anyone* who asks you for a reason for the hope that is in you; yet do it with gentleness and respect, (1 Peter 3:14b-15)

While both positions lay claim to their knowledge of the source behind the origin of life, both cannot be equally true.

Are We Absolutely Sure About That?

We must stress to our listeners that the foundation for truth rests in God. Truth is not a variable. It is not defined by what a person wants to believe about it. Truth about all things, including creation, is neither fluid nor malleable. Truth does not change or vacillate according to majority rule or cultural bent. It is not dependent upon how one chooses to understand truth. Truth does not 'become' truth the moment we choose to accept it as such. Truth is truth, completely independent of our interaction with it. That is because truth is a *universal absolute* that God has set in place. Thus, our conversation will naturally expand to another area: What do we mean when we say, absolute? And the defining continues.

In simple terms, an absolute is something that is perpetually consistent and not subject to ebb under any circumstances. It is the plumb line for which all other things that exist are measured. An absolute is universally valid, used as an indispensible measurement wholly independent of subjectivity.

Today our culture is decrying that we do not live in a world of absolutes; that everything we experience, know, or do is based upon our own inner assessment of the need of the moment. What is true or not true can shift depending upon how we feel at the time or how our decision would best serve us.

People who resolve to live as if there are no absolutes merely demonstrate the extent of our cultural conditioning, coldly rejecting the reality of God, while warming up to the implausibility of evolution. The assertion that there are no absolutes is, in fact, an absolute statement, and is really quite peculiar. As inhabitants of this planet we are subject to absolutes every single day. The earth's atmosphere, air, water, food, heat, and sunlight are just a few examples of the absolutes to which we humans are subject. Ignore or deprive ourselves of any of these and we will perish. Of that we can be absolutely sure!

To continually ignore the evidence, all the while claiming we are free of absolutes, can be illustrated this way: Suppose a professor decides to proctor a math test without an answer guide. Refusing to acknowledge the existence of absolutes in this scenario would make every student's equation and answer on the test equally valid because there is no universal right or wrong with which to compare their work. Their answers would be based upon what they *felt* and *wanted* to be correct, or what they think the professor might want for an answer. As a result, everyone could get an A on the test, even the one who chose not to take the test. In a world free of absolutes, the professor could also choose to give everyone an F if he or she felt like it. In this line of reasoning, an F for everyone would be just as legitimate as an A, because it is based solely upon the professor's subjective preference with no consideration for the necessity of right or wrong.

What seems so silly and absurd in this simple illustration is the very way unbelieving man attempts to live out his life every day, without rules or boundaries. He confidently assures himself that there are no absolute consequences because there is no such thing as an absolute God. He sees accountability for his actions or inactions as irrelevant and threatening.

We should not be content to permit another person to assume that it is entirely possible for two people to harmoniously co-exist in a state of complete contradiction, i.e., relativism, void of absolutes. God is not glorified in muddy waters. By our inactions to define truth in conversation, are we demonstrating that we fail to grasp what is at stake, or that we really aren't that concerned with what the other person believes? In either case, neither is right nor God honoring.

Gently exposing the possibility of escape from one's self-generated world of contradiction, contingency, and relativism can actually place a person on the path to true inner freedom.

For one to become conscious that they don't have to unremittingly fill the role of 'creator-god' in their own little worlds can be a significant stress-reliever, especially in a culture that dogs you to purport that your own world is bigger and better than your neighbor's.

Divine encounters provide a tremendous opportunity to converse with another individual about what is true, why it is true, and why in God, truth is absolute. But in order to converse with confidence, it is imperative that we ourselves be familiar with the evidence God has amply supplied.

Recalibration

In a culture that has demonstrated over and over that it is thoroughly confused about the issue of what is true, God is asking us to do two things:

First, experience the reality of his trustworthiness in our own lives:

> You keep him in perfect peace whose mind is stayed on you, because he trusts in you. Trust in the LORD forever, for the LORD GOD is an everlasting rock. (Isaiah 26:3-4)

> Trust in the LORD with all your heart, and do not lean on your own understanding. In all your ways acknowledge him, and he will make straight your paths. (Proverbs 3:5-6)

Second, openly make known his trustworthiness to those around us:

> For I am not ashamed of the gospel, for it is the power of God for salvation to everyone who believes, to the Jew first and also to the Greek. (Romans 1:16)

> But I am not ashamed, for I know whom I have believed, and I am convinced that he is able to guard until that Day what has been entrusted to me. (2 Timothy 1:12b)

God does not want anyone guessing whether or not he is completely trustworthy. Our bid to make God known to others cannot be based on some inner subjective feeling devoid of his objective truth. That is an inaccurate blueprint from which one can only build a flawed view of God. Subjectivity without objectivity leaves everyone taking an educated guess about God and purports the false assumption that a person may come up with his or her own version of truth. Therefore, it is vital that we work from the assumption of God's established absolutes.

A careless or lackadaisical approach to our pursuit of God is a breeding ground for misunderstanding, misquoting, and misrepresenting our Maker. It is never a good thing to have to 'unteach' a mischaracterization of God. His design is for us to accurately portray him by:

1. Making public *who* he is.
2. Making plain *what* we believe about him.
3. Making plausible *why* we believe him to be trustworthy.

We have a weighty task set before us. God has placed his reputation in our hands and he will hold us accountable for how we handle the evidence. Every single son and daughter of the Most High is an ambassador who has been sent out to make God known, declaring his word and demonstrating that he is truthful in all he says.

The wonderful news is that we don't have to figure all this out on our own.

Jesus has assured his true followers that he will always be by their side to enlighten, empower, and enable.

And behold, I am with you always, to the end of the age. (Matthew 28:20b)

When the Spirit of truth comes, he will guide you into all the truth, for he will not speak on his own authority, but whatever he hears he will speak, and *he will declare to you the things that are to come.* He will glorify me, for *he will take what is mine and declare it to you.* All that the Father has is mine; therefore I said that *he will take what is mine and declare it to you.* (John 16:13-15)

Discussion Questions

1. Why is a proper definition of truth essential?

2. Why are absolutes necessary?

3. What are some presuppositions offered for our existence?

4. What is the difference between a contradiction and an opposing view?

5. Why is it important to be familiar with the evidence God has provided us?

FINAL THOUGHTS

IT'S REALLY ALL ABOUT GOD . . .

the path to real life

There is not a man or woman who doesn't want his or her life to be something more . . . more significant, more fulfilling, to know that he or she has worth. All of us are aware that the demands of this life can be overwhelming at times, even insurmountable in this non-stop world of developing chaos. On the receiving end of the cultural barrage of ever-increasing information and activity, men and women find themselves being forced to react to life rather than living it out with intent. And while sensing the futility, there still remains the fleeting dream; that with a lot of hard work and a little luck, one day things might just level out. Thankfully, God has spoken directly to this approach to life in order to give us an authentic hope.

It is not God's intention to make life hard for us. While life can be problematic, even unmanageable at times, the disappointments and frustrations we experience do not arise out of God's being mean-spirited or uninvolved. God wants us to know that he is not the cause of our problems, agitations, and chaos. He is our solution. Jesus has declared:

> The thief comes only to steal and kill and destroy. *I came that they may have life and have it abundantly.* (John 10:10)

God insists that he is here to help his sons and daughters and not to harm them. He reminds us that the truth to experiencing lasting satisfaction in life cannot be found in a person's focusing his or her energies on their own survival, thus making everything about him or her. No, the key to real meaning is found in the radical decision to start making one's life all about God. True living only begins when we decide to occupy ourselves with the passionate pursuit of God, to make him our number one priority. Listen to the Psalmist:

> "You make known to me the *path of life*; in your presence there is *fullness of joy*; at your right hand are *pleasures forevermore*" (Psalm 16:11).

There is only one genuine journey! The 'path of life' is intended to lead us right into the presence of our Maker. We have the promise that when we wholly devote ourselves to walking that path, God, in turn, will reward us with lasting joy and endless pleasures. The abundance in life that we all so earnestly seek will be apprehended only when we make a conscious decision to be all about him. And it is in that very revelation we learn why we have been created:

> You shall love the LORD your God with all your heart and with all your soul and with all your might. (Deuteronomy 6:5)

Made in the USA
Charleston, SC
17 October 2012